Microsoft Access Answers: Certified Tech Support

Mary Campbell

Osborne **McGraw-Hill**

Berkeley · New York · St. Louis
San Francisco · Auckland · Bogotá
Hamburg · London · Madrid · Mexico
City · Milan · Montreal · New Delhi
Panama City · Paris · São Paulo
Singapore · Sydney · Tokyo · Toronto

Osborne **McGraw-Hill**
2600 Tenth Street, Berkeley, California 94710, USA

For information on software, translations, or book distributors outside of the U.S.A., please write to Osborne McGraw-Hill at the above address.

Microsoft Access Answers: Certified Tech Support

567890 DOC 99876

ISBN 0-07-882069-3

Publisher
Lawrence Levitsky

Acquisitions Editors
Scott Rogers
Joanne Cuthbertson

Editorial Assistant
Kelly Vogel

Project Editors
Claire Splan
Janet Walden

Copy Editor
Jan Jue

Proofreader
Pat Mannion

Indexer
Richard Shrout

Computer Designer
Roberta Steele

Illustrator
Marla Shelasky

Series Design
Marla Shelasky

Quality Control Specialist
Joe Scuderi

Cover Design
Ted Mader & Associates

Contents
at a
Glance

Contents

Foreword

Few things are as frustrating as having a computer problem that you can't solve. Computer users often spend hours trying to find the answer to a *single* software question! That's why the tech support experts at Corporate Software Incorporated (CSI) have teamed up with Osborne/McGraw-Hill to bring you the **Certified Tech Support Series**—books designed to give you all the solutions you need to fix even the most difficult software glitches.

At Corporate Software, we have a dedicated support staff that handles over 200,000 software questions every month. These experts use the latest hardware and software technology to provide answers to every sort of software problem. CSI takes full advantage of the partnerships that we have forged with all major software publishers. Our staff frequently receives the same training that publishers offer their own support representatives and has access to vendor technical resources that are not generally available to the public.

Thus, this series is based on actual *empirical* data. We've drawn on our support expertise and sorted through our vast database of software solutions to find the most important and frequently asked questions for Microsoft Access. These questions have also been checked and rechecked for technical accuracy and are organized in a way that will let you find the answer you need quickly—providing you with a one-stop tech support solution to your software problems.

No longer do you have to spend hours on the phone waiting for someone to answer your tech support question! You are holding the single, most authoritative collection of answers to your software questions available—the next best thing to having a tech support expert by your side.

　　We've helped millions of people solve their software problems. Let us help you.

Randy Burkhart
Senior Vice President, Technology
Corporate Software Inc

Acknowledgments

I would like to thank all the staff at Corporate Software who enthusiastically committed so much time and knowledge to this effort. So many of them spent time on weekends and after hours to search their data banks for the best questions and answers. They also spent untold hours reviewing manuscript and pages and responding to all of our requests for help. Without all of their hard work, this book would not exist. I would like to personally thank each of the following people for their assistance: Kim A., Laura K., Faith K., Phil W., Scott L., Chanel W., and Larry D.

The staff at Osborne was also an important part of this book. Without exception, everyone did more than their share to insure that we met all the important deadlines. I would like to extend special thanks to: Larry Levitsky, Publisher, for the idea to do the series and all of his work with Corporate Software to make the idea a reality; Scott Rogers and Joanne Cuthbertson, Acquisitions Editors, who took the time to read each chapter and made excellent suggestions for improvements; Kelly Vogel, Editorial Assistant, who helped to organize all the components of the project; Claire Splan and Janet Walden, Project Editors, whose handling of this project is as flawless as ever; and all of the Production staff, who each did everything possible to make this book the best source of technical support available.

I would also like to especially thank my assistants, Gabrielle Lawrence and Elizabeth Reinhardt. They contributed extensively to the book's contents and art work. They also proofread the final manuscript to help catch technical and grammatical errors.

Introduction

There is no good time to have a problem with your computer or the software you are using. You are anxious to complete the task you started and do not have time to fumble through a manual looking for an answer that is probably not there anyway. You can forget about the option of a free support call solving your problems since most software vendors now charge as much as $25 to answer a single question. *Microsoft Access Answers: Certified Tech Support* can provide the solution to all of your Access problems. It contains the most frequently asked Access questions along with the solutions to get you back on track quickly. The questions and answers have been extracted from the data banks of Corporate Software, the world's largest supplier of third-party support. Since they answer over 200,000 calls a month from users just like you, odds are high that your problem has plagued others in the past and is already part of their data bank. *Microsoft Access Answers: Certified Tech Support* is the next best thing to having a Corporate Software expert at the desk right next to you. The help you need is available seven days a week, any time you have a problem.

Microsoft Access Answers is organized into 13 chapters. Each chapter contains questions and answers on a specific area of Access. Within each chapter, you will find the questions organized by features of that Access topic. With this organization, you can read through questions and answers on particular topics to familiarize yourself with them before the troubles actually occur. An excellent index makes it easy for you to find what you need even if you are uncertain which chapter would cover the solution.

Throughout the book you will also find the following elements to help you sail smoothly through your Access tasks, whether you are a novice or a veteran user:

- **Frustration Busters:** Special coverage of Access topics that have proven confusing to many users. A few minutes spent reading each of these boxes can help you avoid problems in the first place.

- **Tech Tips and Notes:** Short technical helps that provide additional insight to a topic addressed in one of the questions.

- **Tech Terrors:** Pitfalls you will want to steer clear of.

Top Ten Tech Terrors

In this first chapter, we've presented step-by-step solutions for the top ten technical terrors that you are most likely to run into with Access for Windows. These are problems that thousands of users have encountered. They received expert help from Corporate Software, and now you can, too!

You can probably avoid these tech terrors altogether just by reviewing this chapter now. Later, if any of these terrors should still arise, you'll know just what to do.

When I open my report, I see "#Name?" in some controls. Why can't I see my data?

"#Name?" is the error message that appears in a control when it can't find the data it is supposed to display. *Controls* are the elements of a form or report that can display data. Each control has many properties that define how it works. The Control Source property defines the source of the data that the control displays. If this property is set to a source that Access can't find or which doesn't exist, the "#Name?" error message appears instead of the missing data.

Tech Tip: While the idea behind properties may be confusing at first, it is actually quite simple. Properties modify controls the same way that adjectives modify the meaning of a noun. An adjective can't change the basic definition of the noun, but it does provide more information. Properties can't change the kind of control in your form or report, but they can provide clarifying information, such as what data the control displays.

Figure 1-1 shows a form with several controls that have invalid Control Source property settings. You want these controls to show meaningful data, so you need to make the Control Source

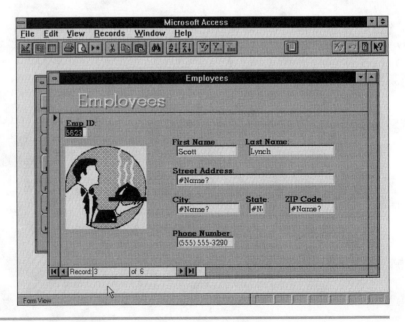

FIGURE 1-1   Form with invalid data

property setting valid. To change the Control Source property setting, switch to the form or report's Design view. To do this, choose Form Design or Report Design from the View menu or click the Design View toolbar button. Select the control displaying #Name?.

Access offers a shortcut for changing the Control Source property's setting. When the form appears in Design view, the Control Source property's current setting usually appears in the control itself. You can edit the text in the control to change this property. If you prefer, open the property sheet by choosing Properties from the View menu, and then move to the Control Source property and edit the setting there.

Tech Tip: You can show either some or all of the properties for a control in the property sheet. To show all of the properties, select All Properties from the drop-down list box. To show a set of related properties, select the appropriate entry in this drop-down list box.

Check the contents of the Control Source property. The current setting may be a mistyped field name or may refer to a field you removed from the table. Set this property to an existing source of data. After you fix the entry, your form or report should work correctly.

Tech Terror: When you rename a field in a table, Access does not update the field name in queries, forms, and reports. You need to modify the queries, forms, and reports where the field appears.

When I try attaching a Microsoft SQL (Structured Query Language) server table, I get the message "Reserved error 7745; there is no message for this error." What does this mean?

This message appears because the Microsoft SQL server is not communicating with the ODBC (Open Database Connectivity) driver, a file Access uses to work with databases created by other database management programs. Run the INSTCAT.SQL script with your Microsoft SQL server to prepare it for communication with the ODBC driver.

Access Setup does not automatically install the INSTCAT.SQL script. Before running it, you need to decompress the file on the

Access Setup Disk 1 and copy it to your hard drive. Use
DECOMP.EXE, on the same disk, to decompress the file. Switch
to the DOS prompt, and then enter **A:\DECOMP.EXE
A:\INSTCAT.SQ_ C:\INSTCAT.SQL**. This copies and
decompresses the INSTCAT.SQ_ file to INSTCAT.SQL on drive C.
Specify different drives or directories as needed.

---

3. All the calculated fields in my query show more decimal places than I want. How do I format them to show fewer decimal places?

The easiest way to limit the number of decimal places displayed
in a field is to set the field's Decimal Places property. To set this
property for any field displaying numbers:

1. Switch to the query's Design view by choosing Query
   Design from the <u>V</u>iew menu, or by clicking the Design
   View toolbar button, shown here:

2. Move to the first field whose decimal places you want
   to limit.

3. Open the property sheet by choosing <u>P</u>roperties from the
   <u>V</u>iew menu, or by clicking the Properties toolbar button
   shown here:

Tech Tip: If you
can't find the
property you want,
change which
properties are listed.
Selecting a different
option in the drop-
down list box at the
top of the property
sheet determines
which properties will
appear.

4. Move to the Format property and choose a format other
   than General. For example, to display dollar amounts,
   choose Currency. If you aren't sure which format to use,
   choose Fixed.

5. Move to the Decimal Places property and enter the
   number of decimal places you want to use.

6. Repeat these steps for each field whose decimal places
   you want to limit.

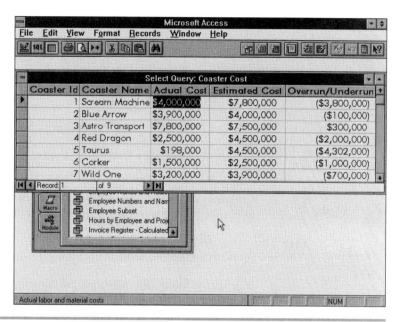

FIGURE 1-2   Query after setting the Decimal Places property

When you switch back to the query's Datasheet view, the fields
for which you set the Decimal Places property display only the
set number of digits after the decimal point. If you set all of your
fields to the Currency format, with 0 decimal places, your query
might look like Figure 1-2.

When I try printing a report, I receive the message "Query is too complex." What's wrong?

You've based your report on a query too complex for Access to
run. Things that can make a query too complex are

- Length of the table or field names
- Number of fields in the query
- Number of expressions used to create calculated fields or
  criteria

Tech Note: You might be confused if you have run your query without receiving this error message. However, creating the report adds one more level of complexity to Access' task. That one level of complexity may be the one that makes the task too complex for Access to complete.

To print your report, you need to simplify your query. To do so:

- Remove unnecessary fields from the query.

- If possible, simplify the expressions in the query.

- Convert complex expressions into user-defined functions and specify the user-defined function in the query.

Tech Tip: User-defined functions are created as procedures in a Module window.

- If possible, break the query into two or more queries.

 When I choose one of the Wizards, I get a message about a compiling error. What's wrong with my Wizards?

Most likely, your Wizards are fine, but the code in your database isn't. Before Access runs any Wizards, it compiles all of the code currently in memory. This includes code stored in the open database and the loaded library databases, such as the one storing

your Wizard. You get an error message when Access encounters errors in the code such as undefined variables or functions, regardless of which database stores the code.

To run the Wizard, find the error in your database and correct it. To do this, open any module in Design view. Then start compiling your modules by choosing Compile Lo<u>a</u>ded Modules from the <u>R</u>un menu. When Access finds the line of code causing the error, it highlights the line in a Module window. Correct the error and the Wizard will run.

6 Why do I get the message "Can't add or change record. Referential integrity rules require a related record in table *'tablename'*" when I try add a record in my form?

When you set up a relationship between the table the form is based on and another table, you chose to enforce referential integrity. Relationships between tables indicate how records in the two tables relate. For example, you could set a one-to-many relationship between the Employee ID field in your Employees table and the Sales Representatives field in your Invoices table. When you enforce referential integrity, Access makes sure that all new and edited records in the tables keep the type of relationship you set. For example, in this one-to-many relationship, you can only enter ID numbers for the Sales Representatives ID field that already exist in the Employee ID field in the Employees table.

When you try to save a record, Access checks to make sure that the record doesn't violate referential integrity. For example, after you enter a record in your Invoices table, Access checks that the entry in the Sales Representatives field already exists in the Employees table. If it doesn't, Access won't save the record and displays the message you saw.

Enforcing referential integrity protects you against in correct entries. If you mistype an employee's ID in the Sales Representatives field, Access stops you. Obviously, your sales representative can't be someone who isn't already an employee. This lets you fix the mistake immediately instead of discovering it much later.

7 Why do I get the message "No permissions for *object*" when trying to work with an object for which I have full permissions?

When you see this message, double-check that you have the necessary permissions for the object. The easiest way to check is as follows:

1. Highlight the database object in the Database window.
2. Choose Print Definition from the File menu.

3. Make sure the Permissions by User and Group check box is selected and select OK.

Access displays a definition of the selected database object, including the permissions assigned to it. If you do have the permissions, this error message is being displayed because of some other problem. There are several possible reasons:

Tech Terror: If your database was encrypted, and your SYSTEM.MDA file is missing or corrupt, you have a serious problem. You can no longer access that data. Unless you backed up a copy of the SYSTEM.MDA file or a copy of the decrypted database, you've just lost it all.

- Your SYSTEM.MDA file may be corrupt, missing, or changed. If something happened to your SYSTEM.MDA file, Access may be unable to locate the permissions information. To fix this problem, you need to replace the SYSTEM.MDA file. Your best option is to restore a backup copy of this file into the directory. If you don't have a backup copy, you can create a new one, and then reassign the permissions. To do this, start the Access Workgroup Administrator by double-clicking its program icon in the Program Manager. Choose Create, enter the necessary information, and select OK. Use the same Workgroup ID that the damaged file had. If the SYSTEM.MDA file was just moved, you don't need to create a new one. You can choose Join in the Access Workgroup Administrator, and then enter the new path to the file.

- The database object itself could be corrupt. A quick solution that often works is to repair and compact the database. Close all databases, and then choose Repair Database from the File menu. Enter the name of the database to repair and select OK. Access will attempt to repair any problems with the database. Then choose Compact Database from the File menu, and supply the same database's name. Compacting a database rearranges its contents so Access can work with the database objects faster; in addition, it removes file space that the database no longer needs. If repairing and compacting the database doesn't work, you may need to use your backup database and reenter all of the data entered since the last backup.

Tech Tip: Don't wait until you cannot get to your data to worry about backups. Back up your important databases frequently, so you can return to a backup copy if the original database becomes irreparably damaged.

What does the "Type mismatch" error mean?

Access compiled one or more procedures in your database. It found a discrepancy between the data type it expects and the data type given to it. Usually this is a result of text and numeric fields becoming mixed up in a calculation or expression.

Access Basic code includes variables and constants that represent values or objects in a database. Variables and constants have a setting that describes the type of data they represent. Errors can occur when Access expects one type of variable or constant (such as text), and is mistakenly provided another type (such as numeric).

When you see this message, Access opens a Module window and highlights the line of Access Basic code causing the problem. Figure 1-3 shows a Module window opened after Access displayed the "Type mismatch" message. This procedure has a type mismatch problem because the first and third arguments for the Mid function are reversed. After Access identifies the source of the error, fix the code and recompile the module.

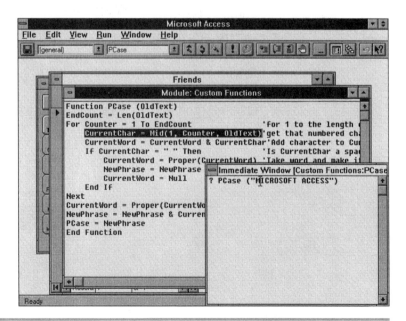

FIGURE 1-3   Access Basic code highlighted to show the location of an error

I tried creating a one-to-many relationship between two tables using Counter fields, but Access won't let me. What can I do?

Access does not let you create a relationship using two Counter fields. The second field must be a Number field with the Field Size property set to Long Integer.

When I try to enter a new record in my form, the message "Recordset is not updatable" appears. What can I do?

You've probably based the form on a query that is not updatable. If you can't edit or add records in a query, then you can't edit or add them using a form based on that query. Queries that aren't updatable include

- Crosstab, pass-through, and union queries
- Queries that calculate totals
- Queries that include attached tables without indexes or primary keys
- Queries for which you do not have permission to update or delete records
- Queries showing multiple tables or queries that aren't joined
- Queries with the Unique Values property set to Yes

Access Basics

Although Access is a powerful database management program, it is designed to be easy to use. Many of the problems encountered with the package occur because of the vast array of features and the new ways that Access provides to use all of the graphical features that Windows offers.

Even in simple tasks such as installation and basic database creation, there are numerous potential problem areas. Some users experience difficulty installing Access on compressed drives. Others find that a database becomes unmanageable with graphics. This chapter provides the answer to these and other basic Access questions, letting you overcome these problems and focus on more advanced options.

FRUSTRATION BUSTERS!

One of the most frustrating aspects of starting to use Access is learning the terms and the concepts behind organizing your data. Whether you are upgrading from another database management program or using one for the first time, you'll find that the following definitions will help you work with Access' features.

In Access, a *database* is a single file that contains your data and all the tools (such as forms and reports) for working with it.

When you open a database, the *Database window* appears and shows the objects in the database. On the left edge of the window, there are six tabs that let you select which objects currently display in the window (see Figure 2-1).

Tables are where you store your raw data. They are arranged like spreadsheets. Each column, or *field*, holds a specific type of information, such as ZIP codes. Each row or *record* contains the information on a specific entity or event, such as a client, patient, or instrument reading.

Queries extract and combine data from tables based on criteria you provide. For example, you can use a query to extract records from the Employee table for every employee who worked overtime in the last week. Queries can also perform actions on a group of data.

Forms are windows that appear on the screen and are used to present data or direct data entry.

Reports are like forms, except that they are meant to be printed, rather than displayed on the screen, and are not used to enter data.

Macros automate tasks and are used to simplify working in Access.

Modules are sheets containing Access Basic code used to program in Access.

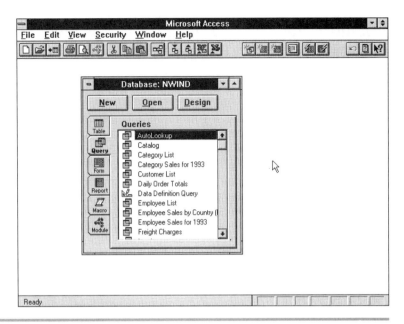

FIGURE 2-1   The Database window

Can I install Access 2.0 on a compressed drive?

Access can only be used on a compressed drive if the
compression ratio is below 1.4 to 1. If the ratio is greater than
1.4 to 1, do not attempt to install Access on your compressed
drive. Check the documentation of your disk compression
program to find out how to determine the ratio. If it is too high,
try installing Access 2.0 on the uncompressed host drive.

My copy of Access 2.0 did not include a Language Reference like the one included with Access 1.0. How can I get a copy of this manual?

Instead of providing the Language
Reference manual, Microsoft provides
the complete text of the language
reference as part of the online help. To
view this information, open the
Contents topic, and click Language
and Technical Reference. You can then
find the information you need.

You can purchase a printed copy of the Language Reference
from Microsoft Corporation. To do so, contact Microsoft's
Product Sales department by calling (800) 426-9400.

I thought my Access application files were corrupt, so I reinstalled Access. However, I still have the same problems. What next?

Actually, what you need to do is go back and reinstall Access a second time. If you try installing Access with a current copy in place, Access Setup simply replaces any missing files. It doesn't replace the existing application files that you believe are corrupt. To replace all of the files, start Access Setup and select Remove All to completely remove your copy of Access. Then reinstall Access using the Setup disks. If you know which files or components of Access are corrupt, you can delete those files, and then start Access Setup and select Reinstall to replace them.

Tech Tip: Use Setup to remove the Access files instead of simply deleting the \ACCESS directory. Many of the files that Access uses aren't installed in the \ACCESS directory. Using Setup removes all the Access program files regardless of their location.

Which networks can Access 2.0 work on?

Access 2.0 supports five networks. These are

- Microsoft LAN Manager
- Microsoft Windows for Workgroups
- Microsoft Windows NT
- Novell version 3.1*x*
- Artisoft LANtastic

I installed Access 2.0 on a system using Windows NT, but I don't have an ODBC icon in the Control Panel. What's wrong?

Access Setup does not create an ODBC Control Panel option when run on a system using Windows NT. This is because the

Control Panel in Windows NT is different from the ones in Microsoft Windows and Windows for Workgroups. However, you can create a program item for the ODBC Administrator by choosing <u>N</u>ew from the Program Manager's <u>F</u>ile menu. The file you want to add is ODBCADM.EXE.

When I tried installing Access 2.0, I got an out-of-memory message even though I have plenty of available memory. What can I do?

First, make sure you actually have enough memory to install or run Access. Switch to the DOS prompt and enter **MEM**. DOS reports on the status of the memory installed on your system, as shown in Figure 2-2. If you have less than 4 megabytes (MB) of memory on your system, you don't have enough memory. You'll need to install more memory before you can install or run Access 2.0.

Tech Tip: Access can run on 4MB of memory, but most people consider its performance inadequate. For Access to run well, you should have 8MB or more of memory on your system.

```
Memory Type        Total   =   Used  +   Free
----------------   -------     -------   -------
Conventional        640K        135K      505K
Upper                 0K          0K        0K
Reserved            128K        128K        0K
Extended (XMS)    3,328K      2,304K    1,024K
----------------   -------     -------   -------
Total memory      4,096K      2,567K    1,529K

Total under 1 MB    640K        135K      505K

Total Expanded (EMS)              1,024K (1,048,576 bytes)
Free Expanded (EMS)               1,024K (1,048,576 bytes)

Largest executable program size    505K (516,896 bytes)
Largest free upper memory block      0K      (0 bytes)
MS-DOS is resident in the high memory area.
```

FIGURE 2-2   MEM displays information about your system's memory

If you have at least 4MB of memory in your system, your problem is that other applications are using the memory you need for Access. To fix this, close all open applications before trying to install Access again. You should routinely close all applications before attempting to install a new one, particularly a Windows one. Other applications may be using files that Access' installation program needs to edit or replace.

If you try to install Access again after closing all other applications and still get an out-of-memory error, you need to set Windows so that it uses less memory. To do this:

1. Open the Windows Setup application, whose program icon is normally found in the Main program group. If the Display line is set to SVGA, choose Change System Settings from the Options menu. Choose VGA from the Display drop-down list box, then select OK, respond to the prompts, and choose Exit from the Options menu. The VGA display driver, which tells your computer how to communicate with the monitor, uses less memory than the more advanced SVGA display driver.

2. Do a *clean boot* to avoid having your computer automatically install any terminate-and-stay-resident (TSR) applications. Performing a clean boot with DOS 6.*x* is easy. Just exit all of your applications, including Windows. Then press the Reset button on your computer or press CTRL+ALT+DEL. When you see the phrase "Starting MS-DOS" on your screen, press F8. When DOS prompts you about executing each command in the AUTOEXEC.BAT and CONFIG.SYS files, type **y** in response to the lines that contain the words HIMEM.SYS, FILES, BUFFERS, and SHELL. Type **n** in response to all other prompts.

   If you are using an earlier version of DOS, perform a clean boot by editing your AUTOEXEC.BAT and CONFIG.SYS files. Add **REM** to the beginning of every line except those that contain HIMEM.SYS, FILES, BUFFERS, and SHELL. Remember to edit these files and remove these REMs after installing Access.

3. After performing a clean boot, start Windows in standard mode by entering **WIN /S** at the DOS prompt while in the \WINDOWS directory. Standard mode uses less

memory than 386 Enhanced mode, which Windows uses by default with a 386- or 486-based computer.

Tech Terror: If you need to use any of these suggestions to install Access, you may find that Access runs out of memory when you use a large database or perform complex operations. While you can install Access by using these techniques, you need to consider adding more memory to your system soon.

If changing the video monitor, performing a clean boot, and starting Windows in standard mode still don't solve the problem, your only solution is to manually expand the files. Start by copying the files from the Setup disks into a directory of your system. Then use DECOMP.EXE, found on the first Setup disk, to expand the compressed files.

How can I set Access to maximize my Database window automatically when I open a database?

You need to create a macro that maximizes the window, and then set this macro to execute automatically when you open the database. To create the macro:

1. Click the Macro tab in the Database window.

2. Click <u>N</u>ew, opening a Macro window.

3. Enter **SendKeys** in the Action column of the first row. This macro action sends keystrokes to Access as if you had typed them.

4. Move to the Keystrokes argument in the bottom half of the window and enter **%-x**. The % represents ALT. ALT+- (hyphen) opens the window's Control-menu box, and *x* chooses Ma<u>x</u>imize from the menu.

5. Move to the Wait argument and enter **No**.

6. Choose <u>S</u>ave from the <u>F</u>ile menu.

7. Enter **AutoExec** as the macro's name and select OK. Access automatically executes any macro named AutoExec when you open its database.

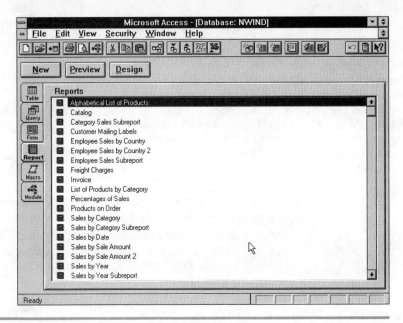

FIGURE 2-3   Maximizing the Database window

Opening the database after creating this macro maximizes the Database window as shown in Figure 2-3.

How do I install Access 2.0 on a network?

To install Access 1.*x* from a server onto a workstation, you started the Setup application using the /n switch. However, you can start Setup normally when installing Access 2.0 onto a network workstation. Simply select the Network installation option while running Setup.

Tech Tip: When you are doing a network administrator's installation of Access, use the /a switch to start Setup.

When I try to open Access, I see the introductory screen, but then Access closes and displays a message saying "*Path* is an invalid path." What can I do?

This message appears when your system database is corrupt or Access can't find it. To fix this, you need to create a new system database. To do this:

1. Start the MS Access Workgroup Administrator by double-clicking its program icon in the Program Manager.

2. Select Create.

3. Enter the information the Workgroup Administrator prompts you for, including your name and your company's name as well as a unique workgroup identifier. Then select OK.

4. Select OK to accept the default filename for the system database.

5. Select Close to exit the Workgroup Administrator.

6. Start Access again.

Tech Terror: If you have to re-create your system database and your database was encrypted, you have lost the data in that database. There is no way to recover the data in a database that is encrypted once the system database storing the permissions is lost. To protect your data, remember to back up your SYSTEM.MDA file as well as your database.

I used to see Cue Cards that helped me do tasks, but they no longer appear. How do I get them back?

At first, the Cue Cards, as shown in Figure 2-4, display automatically when you open a database. If you've turned this feature off, edit Access' initialization file, MSACC20.INI. This file contains many of your customization settings.

Tech Tip: Even if the Cue Cards do not appear automatically, you can still display them by choosing Cue Cards from the Help menu.

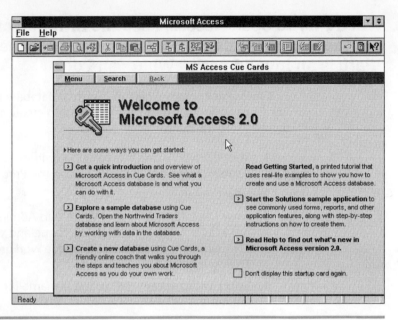

FIGURE 2-4   Cue Cards prompt you about doing specific tasks

To have the Cue Cards display automatically again:

1. Start the Notepad accessory.

2. Open the MSACC20.INI file, stored in the \WINDOWS directory.

3. Move to the section that starts with [Microsoft Access].

4. Find the line that reads Tutorial=0, and change it to read **Tutorial=1**.

5. Save the file and start Access again.

Why do I get the message "Not enough memory on disk" when I'm running a database on a network drive with plenty of room?

It's possible that your temporary directory is not on the network drive. Access stores temporary files in the temporary directory you specify in your AUTOEXEC.BAT file. If this directory is on a drive without much space, such as your local hard drive, you may get this error even though the network drive has adequate free space.

To check your temporary drive:

1. Switch to the DOS prompt. You can do this by exiting Windows, or by double-clicking the MS-DOS Prompt program icon in the Program Manager.

2. Type **SET** at the DOS prompt and press ENTER. DOS displays a series of environmental variables and settings like this:

```
COMSPEC=C:\DOS\COMMAND.COM
PROMPT=$p$g
PATH=C:\ODAPI;C:\WINWORD;C:\DOS;C:\WINWORD;C:\WINDOWS;C:\WORD
TEMP=C:\DOS
windir=C:\WINDOWS
```

3. Look at the line that begins with TEMP=. This is your temporary directory.

Check that this is a valid directory and that there is free space for it. You need to make more free space available in this directory to avoid getting these out-of-memory errors.

Tech Tip: Many other applications use this temporary directory as well. Sometimes, not all of the temporary files are deleted when the applications are closed. Delete any .BAK or .TMP files in this directory to make space. Close all applications before doing this, because you don't want to delete a temporary file that is still in use.

How many network users can have one database open at the same time?

On a network, up to 255 users can be working on the same database at the same time.

What causes an Access database to become corrupt? How can I fix one?

Access database files become corrupt in the same way other files, such as Word documents, become corrupt: power surges, exiting Windows improperly, networks crashing, or viruses. Anything that affects the stability of your computer system can cause one of your files to become corrupt.

Unfortunately, there are no file-restoration programs that can rescue a corrupt Access database. However, even in the most extreme cases of corruption, a database repair should correct the problems. To repair a database:

1. Close any open database.
2. Choose Repair Database from the File menu.
3. Select the database to repair and then select OK.

You may lose some data when repairing a database. A good safeguard against this loss is backing up your database regularly. Since Access does not have a backup feature, just use your favorite backup program.

Can I create a table that shows the definitions of the objects in my database?

In Access 1.x, ANALYZER.MDA created a table containing the information about the objects in your database. Access 2.0 has a new add-in called the Database Documentor that creates a report about the design of your database objects such as tables and reports. To create this table:

1. Open the database you want to document.
2. Choose Add-ins from the File menu.
3. Choose Database Documentor.
4. Select the type of object you want to document from the Object Type drop-down list box.
5. Select the object or objects you want to document.
6. Select Options, set the options you want to include in the table, and select OK.

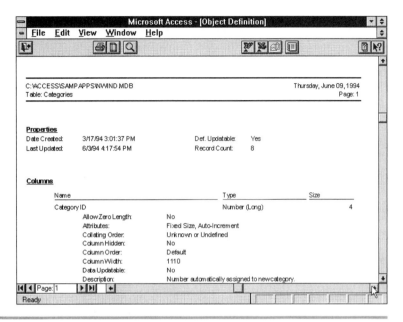

┌───┐
│ ▬   Microsoft Access - [Object Definition]   ▼ ▲ │
│ ▬ <u>F</u>ile <u>E</u>dit <u>V</u>iew <u>W</u>indow <u>H</u>elp   ▲ │
│ ┌──┐   ┌─┬─┬─┐   ┌─┬─┬─┬─┐   ┌─┬─┐ │
│ │↲ │   │🖨│▯│🔍│   │📊│📄│📖│📋│   │?│▶?│ │
│ └──┘   └─┴─┴─┘   └─┴─┴─┴─┘   └─┴─┘ │
│   ▲ │
│   │
│   ──   │
│   C:\ACCESS\SAMPAPPS\NWIND.MDB   Thursday, June 09, 1994 │
│   Table: Categories   Page: 1   │
│   │
│   │
│   <u>Properties</u>   │
│   Date Created: 3/17/94 3:01:37 PM   Def. Updatable: Yes │
│   Last Updated: 6/3/94 4:17:54 PM   Record Count: 8   │
│   │
│   │
│   <u>Columns</u>   │
│   Name   Type   Size   │
│   Category ID   Number (Long)   4   │
│   Allow Zero Length: No   │
│   Attributes: Fixed Size, Auto-Increment   │
│   Collating Order: Unknown or Undefined   │
│   Column Hidden: No   │
│   Column Order: Default   │
│   Column Width: 1110   │
│   Data Updatable: No   │
│   Description: Number automatically assigned to new category. ▼ │
│ ┌─┬─┐ Page: 1 ┌─┬─┐ ┌─┐   ┌──────────────┐   ┌─┐ │
│ │◄│◄│   │►│►│ │+│   │   │   │ │ │
│ └─┴─┘   └─┴─┘ └─┘   └──────────────┘   └─┘ │
│ Ready   │
└───┘

FIGURE 2-5   Creating a report about your database

7. Select OK again, and Access produces a preview of a report documenting the selected database objects as shown in Figure 2-5.

8. Choose Save as <u>T</u>able from the <u>F</u>ile menu. Access creates a table named Object Definition.

9. Click the Close Window button to leave the report.

Tech Tip: To determine the permissions you have for working with an object, follow these steps, but make sure the Per<u>m</u>issions by User and Group check box is selected in the Options dialog box.

Can I print the definitions of my forms, queries, tables, and so on, so I can re-create them if something happens?

Access 2.0 offers you two ways to print the definitions of your database objects. You can print the definitions of several objects at once, or one at a time.

To print the definitions of several objects at once, follow the steps given in the previous question for creating a report with the Database Documentor add-in. Then, instead of creating a table, simply click the Print button in the toolbar and select OK.

To print the definition of a single database object, select the object, and then choose Print Definition from the File menu. Select the definition elements you want to print and select OK. Click the Print toolbar button to print the report about this object.

Can I hide a table so it doesn't appear in the Database window?

If you want to hide a table in the Database window so that other users can't select it, preface the table's name with Usys. For example, if your table's name is Employee, change its name to UsysEmployee. This makes your table into a system object, which Access does not display. System objects are used "behind the scenes" for running Access. Rename an object in the Database window by highlighting it, choosing Rename from the File menu, typing the new name, and selecting OK.

To see this table again later, choose Options from the View menu. Set the Show System Objects option to Yes and select OK. Now you can see the system objects in the Database window. Change this setting back to No when you finish with the table.

I secured my database but I can still see the data. What do I have to do to prevent this?

To prevent others from reading your database with utilities or opening it from other workgroups, encrypt it. When you encrypt a database, you are encoding it using secret codes that only Access can read.

To encrypt an Access database:

1. Close any open databases.

2. Choose Encrypt/Decrypt Database from the File menu.

3. Select the database you want to encrypt and select OK.

4. Specify the name and location for the encrypted database and select OK.

You can use the same name to replace the original database file with the encrypted one. However, you should specify a different name just in case something goes wrong during the encryption process. After you open and test the encrypted database, you can delete the unencrypted one.

I want to reassign permissions in a database, but it was created by someone else. How can I make myself the owner so that I can assign permissions?

To make yourself the owner so you can reassign permissions, you need to import the objects in the database into a new database. To do this:

1. Create a new database by selecting New Database from the File menu.

2. Choose Add-ins from the File menu.

3. Choose Import Database.

4. Select the database you want to import and then select OK.

5. Select OK again when the database finishes importing.

Access imports all objects from the old database into the new one. As the new owner of these objects, you can assign the permissions you want. You may want to delete the old database.

Can I change the owner of my database objects?

You can assign ownership of objects within a database. To do so:

Tech Tip: You can select several objects in the Object list box. Select consecutive objects by selecting the first one, pressing SHIFT, and moving to the last one using the arrow keys or the mouse.

1. Choose <u>C</u>hange Owner from the <u>S</u>ecurity menu while in the Database window.

2. Select the type of object from the Object <u>T</u>ype drop-down list box, and then select the object from the <u>O</u>bject list box.

3. Select a new owner from the <u>N</u>ew Owner drop-down list box.

4. Select OK.

> **Tech Note:** You cannot change the owner of the entire database using the steps given here. To do that, follow the steps given for the previous question.

Why does my file size increase so much when I embed or link graphics?

Your database's size often increases by more than the size of the graphic file you embed or link. This is because Access can only display bitmap pictures. However, Access can use many other graphic formats. When you insert a nonbitmap graphic, Access creates and stores a bitmap image of it. This bitmap is what you actually see in your forms and reports.

When you simply embed a bitmap image, your database file increases by the size of the bitmap file. When you link a bitmap image into Access, it stores both the bitmap picture and the link itself, so the database file is somewhat larger.

When you embed or link a nonbitmap graphic image, the size increase is more dramatic. For example, suppose you link a 100K graphic file in the .JPG format into an Access database. Your database file grows by nearly 2MB. The database must store the 100K image, the bitmap copy of the .JPG file, and the data required for the link.

Tech Note: You can use the Windows Object Packager accessory to store only the link to the graphic image, which saves lots of room. However, if you use the Object Packager, you won't see the graphic image in Access, just the icon you assign with the Object Packager.

I have two files in my directory with the name I assigned to my database. Which one is my database?

The file with the .MDB extension is the database file itself. The file with the .LDB extension is a file that stores record-locking information. Record locking sets which user controls data in Access tables. If you are working in a multiuser or network environment, you'll find that each user who opens the database has an entry in the .LDB file.

Access uses the data in this .LDB file to determine which records are locked and which user has locked them. This enables Access to prevent file-contention errors or corruption of the database by multiple users. The .LDB file is created automatically when you open your Access database file. If you are working in a single-user environment, where no one else can open the database at the same time you do, delete this file to clear up space.

Can I create a custom menu bar that appears when I open a form or report?

Yes, you can change the Access menus you see when working on a form or report. You change them by attaching a macro that creates a custom menu bar to the form or report's MenuBar property. The easiest way to create a custom menu bar macro is to use the Menu Builder. Since these menus are created by macros, see Chapter 11, "Built-In Functions and Macros," for more information about macros in general and about creating menus.

Tech Tip: Access property names frequently consist of several words run together, as in MenuBar. However, Access usually adds spaces to a property name when it's displayed in a dialog box to make it easier to read. When you type a property name for any purpose in Access, type it without the spaces.

I just opened Access, and none of the toolbars appears. How can I get them back?

You've probably turned off the built-in toolbars accidentally. To turn them back on, choose <u>O</u>ptions from the <u>V</u>iew menu. Set the Built-In Toolbars Available option to Yes and select OK. The toolbars should reappear.

If a toolbar doesn't appear, you've probably hidden the one that should—especially if you can see toolbars some of the time, as when you are working with a form. To display a toolbar:

1. Choose Tool<u>b</u>ars from the <u>V</u>iew menu.

2. Highlight the toolbar you want to see in the list and select <u>S</u>how.

3. Choose Close to leave the dialog box.

 ## When I open a form, the toolbox does not appear. I can't select this option from the <u>V</u>iew menu. How can I get my toolbox back?

In Access 2.0, the toolbox that appears when you are in a form or report's Design view is a toolbar. If you cannot select <u>T</u>oolbox from the <u>V</u>iew menu, you've made the built-in toolbars unavailable at some point. Make them available by choosing <u>O</u>ptions from the <u>V</u>iew menu. Set the Built-In Toolbars Available option to Yes and select OK.

You can then select <u>T</u>oolbox from the <u>V</u>iew menu to display it.

 ## Can I change the picture or text on the toolbar buttons?

You can change the face of buttons on your custom toolbars or on the built-in toolbars. To do so:

1. Choose Tool<u>b</u>ars from the <u>V</u>iew menu, or right-click the mouse on a toolbar.

2. Choose <u>C</u>ustomize.

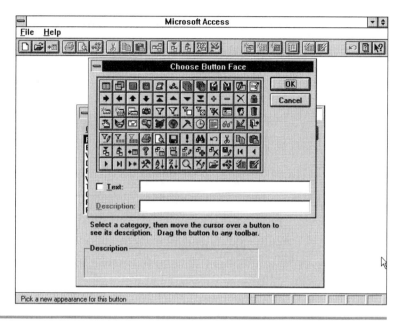

FIGURE 2-6   Access offers a wide variety of bitmap images to use on button faces

3. Right-click the mouse on the button whose face you want to change and pick Choose Button Face from the shortcut menu.

4. Select one of the bitmap images supplied, as shown in Figure 2-6, or enter the text that is to appear on the button.

5. Select OK.

Can Access dial a phone number?

You can have Access dial a phone number if you have a Hayes-compatible modem attached to your system. Access' AutoDialer can dial a phone number from a selected record. To use the AutoDialer, you first need to add the AutoDialer button, shown here, to a toolbar. This button is in the Records category in the Customize Toolbars dialog box. Once you've added the button, select a phone number or move to the field containing it, and click the AutoDialer button, displaying the dialog box shown here:

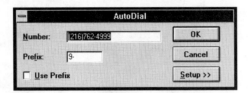

Check that the number is correct, adding any prefixes you might need to dial out from the phone system you are using, and select OK.

Can I edit modules stored in library databases?

To edit the modules of a library database, alter the MSACC20.INI file, which contains many of Access 2.0's default settings. To do this:

1. Close Access.

2. Switch to the Notepad accessory, and open the MSACC20.INI file saved in the \WINDOWS directory.

3. Move to the section headed by [Options] and enter the following line.

```
debuglibraries=true
```

Tech Tip: Check this section to see if the line already appears with a "false" setting. If it does, you can just change the setting to "true."

4. Save the edited MSACC20.INI file and open Access again.

Access now lets you edit modules saved in library databases. To do so, open a Module window for one of your databases and choose Procedures from the View menu. Select a library database from the Databases drop-down list box, and then choose the module and procedure to modify from the Modules and the Procedures list boxes.

How can I mail a copy of database documentation?

You cannot select Send from the File menu when looking at an object definition report. Because of the way Microsoft Mail works, Access cannot mail an object definition report—Access cannot attach the subreports that make up parts of the object definition report. To get around this limitation, print the report and use the Print to File option. This saves the report as a file that you can attach in Microsoft Mail.

What does the toolbar button with the funny looking E do?

Actually, the toolbar button doesn't show an E, but a capital sigma ($\sum$), the mathematical symbol for totals, as you can see here. This button should appear when you are designing a query. Clicking this button either hides or displays the Totals row of the QBE grid. This toolbar button is the equivalent of selecting Totals from the View menu.

What does Send on the File menu do, and why is it dimmed?

The Send command in the File menu saves the output of your database object to a file and attaches that file to an e-mail message. If it's dimmed on your system, then you do not have an Access-supported e-mail system installed. If you installed your e-mail system after Access, you may have to reinstall the Access program files for Access to recognize that the e-mail program is available.

Tech Tip: You can send any type of database object except macros.

Is there a shortcut for entering the current date and time?

Yes, Access has shortcut keys for entering the current date and time.

- Press CTRL+; (semicolon) to enter the current date.
- Press CTRL+: (colon) to enter the current time.

Every time I choose one of the Wizards, I get the message "Can't find Wizard, or there is a syntax error in the Declarations section of an Access Basic module. Check the [Libraries] section of MSACC20.INI for required Wizard libraries, and compile all Access Basic modules in the database." What's wrong with my Wizards?

Most likely, your Wizards are fine, but the code in your database isn't. Before Access runs any code, it compiles all of the code currently in memory. This includes code stored in the open database and the loaded library databases, such as the one storing your Wizard. You get this error message whenever Access encounters errors in the code, regardless of the database storing it.

To run the Wizard, find the error in your database and correct it. To do this, open any module in Design view. Then start compiling your modules by choosing Compile Loaded Modules from the Run menu. When Access finds the line of code causing the error, it highlights the line in a Module window. Correct the error and the Wizard will run.

Why does the picture I inserted as an OLE (Object Linking and Embedding) object look different than in its original application?

The application you created the picture with probably used a larger palette of colors than Access uses. By default, Access uses a 16-color palette. If the other application used more colors to create the image, the original picture will have a greater degree of clarity.

To improve the image's appearance in Access, use a different palette of colors. For example, you may want to use 256 colors to display the image. To do this, change the PaletteSource property of the form or report to identify a bitmap file that provides another palette of colors. Enter the full path name for a file whose palette you want to adopt. For example, if you want the form or report to use a 256-color palette, enter the complete path name to one of the Windows bitmap files that uses 256 colors, as in **C:\WINDOWS\256COLOR.BMP**. Now Access uses the 256-color palette from this file instead of the default Access 16-color palette. The PaletteSource property changes to Custom.

I pressed SHIFT+F2, but the Zoom box did not appear. Why?

There are three possible reasons for a zoom box not appearing when you press SHIFT+F2:

- *Low system resources* Try closing other open applications to free some system resources.

- *A damaged .LDB file* The .LDB file that contains information about record locking may have been corrupted. Close the database and delete the .LDB file in your \ACCESS directory. Access re-creates the file using default settings.

■ *Syntax errors in a module* If you see the message "Access Basic compile error. View error in context?" when you try to open the Zoom box, this is the problem. Open the Module window and choose Compile Lo<u>a</u>ded Modules from the <u>R</u>un menu. Access compiles the modules and displays any lines that cause errors. After you fix your code, the Zoom box should work again.

Can I use a variety of language conventions for my database?

No, you cannot. The language conventions used for currency, list separators, date and time formats, and other settings are set by Windows' Control Panel. The same settings are used by all Windows applications. You can only select one language at a time in Windows. Therefore, you can only use one set of language conventions in Access at a time.

Can I get Access to ignore a key such as F1?

Yes, you can disable one of the keys so that other users cannot use them in your database. This is useful in an application where you want to limit the user's options. To do this, create an AutoKeys macro that tells Access what to do when you press a specific key. The AutoKeys macro executes automatically when you open a database. You disable a key by telling Access to do nothing when the key is pressed.

To create an AutoKeys macro:

1. Create a macro group with the name AutoKeys.

2. Choose <u>M</u>acro Names from the <u>V</u>iew menu to display the Macro Name column if you do not already see it.

3. Assign macro names using the SendKeys code of the key you want to disable.

4. Add the SendKeys action and leave the Keystrokes argument empty.

5. Close and save the macro group.

6. Save and close the database.

The next time you open the database, Access performs the AutoKeys macro. The effect of the AutoKeys macro remains as long as the database is open.

For example, you could create an AutoKeys macro to disable the F1 key. Enter **{F1}** in the Macro Name column, and **SendKeys** in the Action column. Leave the Keystrokes argument for the SendKeys action empty. The next time you open the database, Access will perform this macro every time you press F1. Since the Keystrokes argument is empty, no keystroke is sent to Access. Therefore, pressing F1 has no effect.

I am trying to install Access 2.0 on a Novell 3.1x network by starting Setup using SETUP /A to install it onto the server. When I get to the last Setup disk, I get a message saying that the SETUP.INI file is not updatable. I checked the file and found it was read-only. I changed it back and ran Setup again, but got the same error again. So how do I install Access?

The problem is that there is a line in the [Netware Dos Requester] section of Novell's NET.CFG file that reads

```
Read Only Compatibility=On
```

To install Access you need to change this line to read

```
Read Only Compatibility=Off
```

If you are using an earlier version of Novell and encounter this error when installing Access, you can change the same line in the SHELL.CFG file instead of in the NET.CFG file.

Can I use Windows' EXPAND.EXE to expand a file from the Access Setup disks?

No, you cannot use EXPAND to expand the compressed files on Access' Setup disks. To manually expand one of these files, use DECOMP.EXE, found on the first Access Setup disk. To use this program, enter **DECOMP *sourcefile destinationfile*** at the DOS prompt. *Sourcefile* is the file on the Setup disk that you want to expand, and *destinationfile* is the full path name for the file after expansion. For example, to expand the ODBC.DL_ file on the Setup disks, you might enter **DECOMP A:\ODBC.DL_ C:\WINDOWS\SYSTEM\ODBC.DLL** and press ENTER.

Tech Tip: Make sure you use the correct file extension when expanding the program files. Since Access expects to find certain file extensions, misnaming a file can cause Access not to run correctly.

What is the default password for the Admin user account?

The default password for the Admin user account, and all other accounts, is a zero-length string, which is a string containing no characters. To enter a zero-length string, type "" with no space between the quotes. To set a password, choose Change Password from the Security menu and enter a password in the New Password text box. Enter it again in the Verify text box and select OK.

What is the SETUP.STF file?

Access uses the SETUP.STF file to do automated installations for network workstations on a network. These files provide the responses to the Setup application, allowing the network administrator to ensure that Access is set up the same way on every workstation. To use this installation script, start Setup using the /q switch, as in **SETUP /Q**. This makes Setup use the SETUP.STF file to set the Setup options.

Creating Tables

Tables are the heart of your database—they are objects that store all of your data. You need tables before creating other objects such as forms and reports.

You need to carefully plan your tables and the data they contain. The Frustration Busters box that follows explains some basic design steps which will enable you to create tables that match your needs. You should spend more time than you initially think is necessary on the planning stage as it will save time in later phases.

FRUSTRATION BUSTERS!

The first step in creating a database is to plan its design. You need to know exactly what information you want in your database. To determine the data to store, review any printed forms and reports you might have, recording each piece of information used. If this is for your office, ask other employees what kind of information they need to store or retrieve. Remember to consider future needs as well as current ones. Will your data needs change if your company grows? Don't rush this process—time saved by cutting corners here will only cost you later.

After you've figured out what information you need, you should break this information into logical groups. For example, after finding all the information that everyone in your company wants recorded, you can start breaking it up into sets like "Client Data," "Employee Data," and "Manufacturing Data." These sets are the tables you will create.

Try to avoid duplicating information in multiple tables. If you've already decided to store client names and addresses in the Client table, don't include them in another table like Orders. You can define a relationship between the tables to get client addresses rather than duplicate them in an Orders table.

You should also avoid duplicating information within a table. For example, when you record the hours your employees worked every week, you don't want to enter the complete employee name and address each week. That's a waste of time. Instead, create an employee ID number, and enter the ID number for the weekly time records. This employee ID can link to your table of Employee information so the name and address are available without repeating it in each record.

After you arrange all of your tables and define relationships, make sure that you check one last time with anyone else who uses the database. You want to avoid editing the tables' design after you enter data.

What is a table in Access?

A *table* is the object where you store your data. When you create a table, you define the *fields* used for data storage. Each field contains a single type of information, such as an address, a name, or a phone number. Tables can contain hundreds of thousands of records, which are complete sets of information on a single entity. For example, you might have a complete record for each client, including entries in the name, address, and phone number fields. When displayed in Datasheet view, tables have a column and row layout, as shown in Figure 3-1. Each column is a field, and each row is a record.

To create a table:

1. Select the Table tab in the Database window.

2. Select New.

3. Select New Table to open a Table window in Design view, as shown in Figure 3-2. If you select Table Wizards instead, Access starts a Wizard that walks you through the

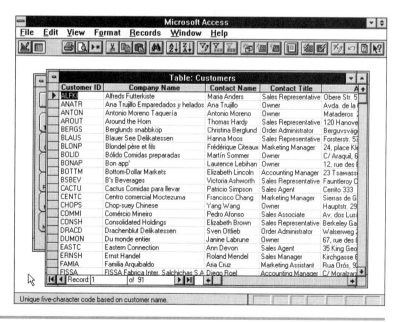

FIGURE 3-1   The Datasheet view of a table

process of creating a table. This Wizard provides sample tables to use as the basis of your own.

4. On each line of the top half of the Table window, enter the name of a field, its data type, and a longer description to help you identify the field. Keep your field names short to make them easier to use later.

5. The properties for each field appear in the bottom half of the Table window. You can move between the top and bottom panes by pressing F6. Move to the box for the property you want to change and enter the new setting.

6. Create a primary key, which is a field or combination of fields that is unique for each record in the table. Click the selector, the small box at the beginning of the row for that field. Then, click the Set Primary Key toolbar button, shown here, or choose Set Primary Key from the Edit menu.

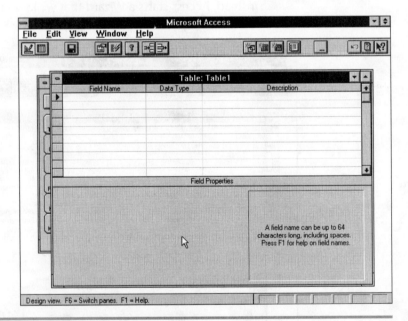

FIGURE 3-2   A new Table window in Design view

7. When you finish, select <u>S</u>ave from the <u>F</u>ile menu. Enter a name for the table and select OK. If you didn't create a primary key before, Access prompts you about creating one now. Select <u>Y</u>es to have Access create a Counter field and make it the primary key, or <u>N</u>o to avoid creating a primary key.

How long can my table name be?

Your table name can be up to 64 characters long. The name should be unique and meaningful, but short enough to make it easy to type later.

Tech Tip: The 64-character limit applies to other objects in Access, including field names and control names.

How large can my table become?

A table can contain an unlimited number of records, but it can be no larger than 1 gigabyte (Gb). Since the 1Gb limit applies to the database as well, a table this large would be the only object in the entire database. Some computer systems may not have sufficient disk space to save such a file or enough memory to open it. You might want to consider splitting a large one into smaller tables.

Another possible limit for tables is the number of fields. A table is limited to 255 fields.

Tech Tip: You can get around the 1Gb limit by attaching large tables.

What are the different types of fields?

Access has eight types of fields to store specific types of data. These include the following:

Data Type	Size	Contains	Limitations
Counter	4 bytes	An integer that Access automatically increments for each new record	Only one in each table
Currency	8 bytes	A number representing a sum of money, using two decimal places	
Date/Time	8 bytes	A date or time	
Memo	Up to 64,000 bytes	Longer text entries	Cannot be used to index a table
Number	1 to 8 bytes	Numeric values	
OLE Object	Up to 1Gb	OLE objects including graphs, pictures, and binary objects	Cannot be used to index a table
Text	Up to 255 bytes	Shorter text entries	
Yes/No	1 bit	Yes or No Values	

In addition to these field types, you can set the Field Size property to specify how many characters a Text field can contain or the range of numbers that a Number field can contain. For example, if you know that a Text field is going to contain first names, you may want to set its Field Size property to 15. You are unlikely to encounter a first name of more than 15 characters.

When you set the Field Size property for a Number field, you can choose one of five field sizes. These field sizes, storage ranges, and storage requirements are as follows:

Field Size	Storage Range	Maximum Decimal Places	Storage Bytes
Byte	0 to 255	0	1
Double	-1.797×10^{308} to 1.797×10^{308}	15	8
Integer	-32,768 to 32,767	0	2
Long Integer	-2,147,483,648 to 2,147,483,647	0	4
Single	-3.4×10^{38} to 3.4×10^{38}	7	4

Tech Terror: By default, the Field Size property for a Text field is 50. If you will have longer entries, change this property to allow more characters. If a Text field is too small, you can make it larger. If you make a Text field smaller after entering data, you may lose data as the long entries in the field are shortened.

What is the difference between an input mask and a format?

Both input masks and formats affect the way data appears in a table in Datasheet view. However, they serve very different purposes.

The Format property setting affects the data in the field once it is entered. It changes how the data displays and can make it easier to read. For example, if you apply the Long Date format to a Date/Time field, a date of 11/24/94 displays as "Thursday, November 24, 1994."

An Input Mask property actually restricts the type of entry you can make in the field. As you begin to make an entry, a template appears indicating the entry needed. This template can also format the entry to make it easier to interpret. For example, if you start to make an entry in a phone number field with an input mask, it might look like this:

Table: Employees				
Street Address	**City**	**State**	**ZIP Code**	**Phone Number**
123 Elm St.	Akron	OH	44302-1506	(2█) __-____

The underscores (_) you see here are placeholders for entries. The hyphen and the parentheses make the phone number entries easier to read.

In creating an input mask, you use placeholder characters for entries. Some placeholder characters allow users to enter a character, digit, or text, while other placeholder characters require an entry. For example, you might use a placeholder character that requires an entry for each of the ten positions in the phone number.

What field types can use input masks?

You can add an input mask to Text, Number, Date/Time, or Currency data type fields.

What's the difference between null and a zero-length string?

When you don't make an entry in a Number or Text type field, that field is *null* for that record. Null simply means that nothing at all was entered. A zero-length string is actually an entry in a Text or Memo type field that doesn't contain anything. When you enter a zero-length string, you type "" without a space between the quotes.

You can prevent users from entering zero-length fields by setting the AllowZeroLength property to No. If you do this and set the Required property for the field to Yes, you can force all users to make meaningful entries in this field. If you set the Required property for the field to Yes and the AllowZeroLength property to Yes, users have to make a zero-length entry if they don't have another entry to make. They cannot leave the record without making an entry in this field. If the Required property for the field is set to No, you are allowing users to leave the field blank, making it null.

You can use the difference between null and a zero-length string to distinguish between data that doesn't exist and data you just don't have yet. For example, set the Required property for a field containing middle names to No and the AllowZeroLength property to Yes. Have users enter a zero-length field when they know that the person has no middle name. Have them make no entry if they either don't know whether the person has a middle name or don't know what that name is.

Can I change the starting value of a Counter type field?

Yes, you can change the starting number for a Counter type field. However, the process is fairly complicated. To do this:

1. Create the first table that contains the Counter type field that you want to start on another number. Don't enter any records.

2. Create a second table with a single Long Integer Number type field that has the same name as the Counter field in the first table.

3. Create a record in the second table by entering a number one less than the number you want to start the Counter field in the first table. For example, if you want to start the Counter field with 1000, enter **999** in the Number field of the second table.

4. Create an append query to append the one record in the second table to the first table and run it.

Tech Tip: See Chapters 5 and 6 for tips about working with queries.

After appending the record from the second table to the first, you can delete the second table and start entering data in the first table.

How can I display the entries in my Yes/No type field as Affirmative and Negative using different colors for each?

You can change how the values in the Yes/No field display by changing the Format property setting for the field. For example, you can enter **"Affirmative"[Black];"Negative" [Red]** to display a black Affirmative for Yes and a red Negative for No. You enclose the text you want to display in place of Yes and No in quotation marks. The colors appear in brackets to indicate that they are colors rather than text to display.

Can I display Text field entries all in uppercase no matter how they are entered?

You can control the case in which table entries display by setting the Format property for that field. In Design view, you need to choose the field, and then move to its Format property, displayed in the lower half of the window. Enter > for this property to force all entries to display in all uppercase, or < to have all entries display in all lowercase. If you use the > setting, the field might look like the Customer ID shown in Figure 3-3.

Tech Tip: You can use the same characters in the Format property of a control in a form or report to control how text displays in these objects.

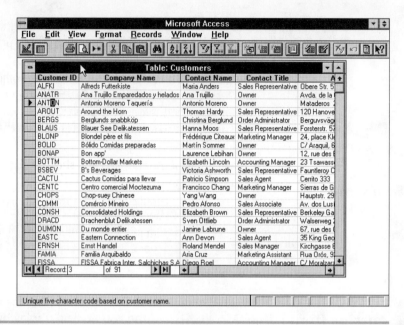

FIGURE 3-3   Using a > Format property for a Text field

Can I display negative numbers enclosed in parentheses, while positive numbers display normally?

You can create a custom format to display negative numbers in parentheses. Custom formats are created with special symbols that indicate what can appear in the field. You enter this custom format as the setting for the Format property for the field.

Table 3-1 lists the special symbols that can create a custom format for a Number field.

Symbol	Effect
"*xxx*"	Displays the characters between the quotation marks, without interpreting them as symbols
\	Displays the character after the backslash without interpreting it as a character. For example "N/A" and \N\/\A both display N/A
0	Displays a digit if one is entered or a zero if one isn't
#	Displays a digit if one is entered or a blank if one isn't
.	Marks the location of the decimal point
%	Multiplies the entry by 100 and displays a % after it
,	Inserts a thousands separator
E- or e-	Shows the number using scientific notation with a - for negative exponents and nothing in front of positive ones
E+ or e+	Shows the number using scientific format with a - for negative exponents and + for positive ones
-	Displays the hyphen as a hyphen
+	Displays the plus sign as a plus sign
$	Displays the dollar sign as a dollar sign
()	Displays the parentheses as parentheses
[*color*]	Displays the number using the color given. You can use Black, Blue, Green, Cyan, Red, Magenta, Yellow, and White
*	Fills the field with the following characters

TABLE 3-1   Symbols for creating custom formats for number type fields

A custom format can have up to four parts. Each part is separated by a semicolon. The first part of the format sets how positive numbers display, the second sets how negative numbers display, the third sets how zeros display, and the fourth determines the appearance of a null field. You do not have to enter all four parts. If you only enter one part, all numbers use that format, while if you enter two parts, zeros and nulls display using the setting for positive numbers.

For example, to display negative numbers in parentheses, you can enter **#,###;(#,###)** as the setting of the Format property of a Number field. This format displays numbers as shown here:

Date	Balance	Administrator	Notes
6/2/95	(1,239)	Phil Walsh	Kim threw a surprise office party to celebrate the Johnson project close
6/9/95	219	Scott Lynch	
6/16/95	(193)	Chanel Ward	
6/23/95	12	Larry Ward	
6/30/95	(340)	Kim Agricola	Larry took accounting team to lunch
7/7/95	320	Faith Kleinert	

Table: PettyCashDrawer — Record: 6 of 6

I want the phone numbers to display the parentheses and dash. How do I do this?

You can change the format to add parentheses and the dash. To create this custom format, you'll use a series of symbols that indicate how to display the data. Text fields, such as your Phone Number field, have several unique symbols for creating custom formats. You can also use other symbols that are available to all types of fields. The available symbols are shown in Table 3-2.

Use	To
<	Display all characters as lowercase
>	Display all characters as uppercase
!	Fill the field from left to right rather than right to left
@	Display an entered character or a space
&	Display an entered character or leave the position empty
[color]	Display the text in a specific color
\	Display the following character literally rather than interpreting as a symbol
*	Fill the field with the following character
a space	Insert a space in the field
""	Enclose text to display literally instead of interpreting as symbols

TABLE 3-2   Symbols for creating custom formats for any field type

For example, to change how your Phone Number field displays the entered phone numbers:

1. Open the table in Design view and choose your Phone Number field.

2. Move to the Format property in the lower half of the window.

3. Enter **(&&&)&&&-&&&&**.

 ## How can I format a field to display a ZIP+4 code?

You can use either an input mask or a format. With an input mask, Access prompts you for the correct data by showing a template in the Datasheet view. Whichever solution you choose, you must make sure that the field to contain this extended ZIP code is a Text type field. Either solution is made by switching to the Design view, moving to the field, and changing one of the properties.

- To add an input mask for the field, move to the Input Mask property. Then click the Build button at the end of the line. Select the standard ZIP code input mask and Next twice. Select whether you want the data stored with the hyphen or not, and then select Next. Select Finish to add the input mask to the Input Mask property.

- If you choose to use a format for the field, move to the Format property and enter **!@@@@@-@@@@**.

 ## Can fields in my table be based on calculations involving other fields?

No, you cannot base fields in your table on the contents of other fields. In Access, tables hold raw data, not formulas or calculations. If you want to display the results of a formula using other fields in the record, you need to create a query with a calculated field or a form or report with a calculated control.

What field types can I index?

You can index Text, Number, Date/Time, Currency, Counter, and Yes/No fields. Indexes are used to sort or search for data in a field quickly. You want to create indexes that order your records the way you need to access your data. For example, if you often sort your table by department number, then create an index for the department number field.

Tech Terror: Don't create too many indexes for a single table. Indexes slow down editing or entering new records, so you don't want to have too many of them.

To create a one-field index:

1. Select the field you want to index.

2. Press F6 to move to the field's properties.

3. Set the Indexed property to Yes (Duplicates OK) if you want to allow duplicate entries in this field, or Yes (No Duplicates) if you want to keep this field unique for each record.

To create a multiple field index:

1. Choose Indexes from the View menu, or click the Indexes toolbar button, shown here:

2. Enter the name for the index in the Index Name column.

3. Enter the name of the first field in the Field Name column next to the name of the index.

4. In the Field Name column below the first field, enter the name of the second field in the index. Continue this until you've added all of the fields you want to index by, as shown here:

Index Name	Field Name	Sort Order	
🔑 PrimaryKey	Emp ID	Ascending	
Address	State	Ascending	
	City	Ascending	
▶	Street Address	Ascending	

Indexes: Employees

Index Properties

5. Close the Indexes window.

What is a primary key?

A *primary key* is a special type of index that uniquely identifies each record. A primary key can use one or more fields, but must be unique for each record. Access will not let you enter a second record using the same primary key. Primary keys also play a role in setting up relationships between tables.

To create a single field primary key, click the selector in front of the field name in the table's Design view. Click the Set Primary Key button, shown here, or choose <u>S</u>et Primary Key from the <u>E</u>dit menu. A key icon appears in the selector as shown here:

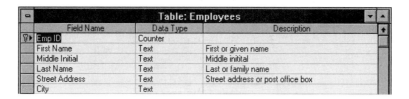

Field Name	Data Type	Description
🔑 ▶ Emp ID	Counter	
First Name	Text	First or given name
Middle Initial	Text	Middle initital
Last Name	Text	Last or family name
Street Address	Text	Street address or post office box
City	Text	

Table: Employees

If you need to create a multiple-field primary key, press CTRL while clicking each of the selectors so you can select all of them, and then follow the same steps.

How do I remove the primary key?

To change which field or fields are used as the primary key, you can remove a primary key from a table. First, you need to make sure the primary key field is not used as the link to relate this table to another table. Access will not let you remove the primary key when it is used to create the relationship between two tables.

To remove the primary key, look at the table in Design view. Open the Indexes window by choosing Indexes from the View menu, or by clicking the Indexes toolbar button. Move to the PrimaryKey row and select the row by clicking its selector. Press DEL to delete the row. Close this window. You can also move to the Field Name column for the PrimaryKey row, and enter the field you now want to serve as the primary key.

I want to use | (pipe or vertical bar) as the default value for a field, but when I try, Access displays the message "Invalid use of vertical bars." What can I do?

The only way to use the vertical bar (pipe) in the Default Value property is to use the Chr(124) function. 124 is the ANSI number that creates the vertical-bar character. If you try to include it by itself or inside quote marks, you will receive an error message.

For example, if you want the default value for a field to be on | off, you can concatenate the text with the Chr() function by entering **"on "& Chr(124) &" off"**.

How can I right-align entries in a text field?

Right-aligning Text and Memo fields is as simple as changing the field's Format property. Display the table's design and move to the field you want to right-align. Switch to the bottom half of the window and type * for the Format property. This change fills the entry's display with spaces. It also

Chapter 3 *Creating Tables*

right-aligns the entry. Fields that have a Format property are right-aligned unless you include the ! alignment character for left alignment. When you save the table's design changes, you will see that your modified fields are right-aligned.

Tech Tip: The alignment of any field's entry can easily be set in forms and reports. Use the alignment options in these objects to change how the data displays.

Working with Tables

4

Tables, the database objects that store your data, are the heart of your database. In the last chapter, you learned about the solutions for creating tables. In this chapter, your questions about working with your tables are answered. When you have problems with entering, finding, or formatting data, here's where you will find the answers.

If you have never worked with a relational database, understanding table relationships is an important first step to problem prevention. See the following Frustration Busters box for an explanation of the relationships between tables.

FRUSTRATION BUSTERS!

In a database, there are three ways to relate tables. Tables can have a one-to-one, one-to-many, or many-to-many relationship. Access only allows the first two. You can redesign your many-to-many relationships to use one-to-many relationships.

The first step is understanding which table is primary and which tables are related to it. The *primary* table is the most important table in a relationship. The *related* table is associated with it. For example, you can create a relationship between the Employee table and a Projects table that indicates the employee who is leading a specific project. In this case, the Employee table is the primary table, and the Projects table is the related table. By relating the two tables, you need to store an Employee ID only in the Projects table. Other data needed on project reports, such as the leader's name, can be obtained from the Employee table.

A *one-to-one* relationship exists when each record in the related table corresponds to only one record in the primary table. One-to-one relationships are usually a bad idea, because they waste space. If you have a one-to-one relationship, you could just add the fields in the related table to the primary table and make one larger table. However, situations do exist where a one-to-one relationship makes sense. For example, the home addresses and job titles of your employees do not require the same security as payroll information. Since you can create separate Employee and Payroll tables, you can apply greater security to the Payroll table.

A *one-to-many* relationship is the most common type of relationship used in a database. In a one-to-many relationship, each record in the primary table corresponds to several records in the related table. However, each record in the related table corresponds to only one in the primary table. For example, you can have a one-to-many relationship between your Client and Invoice Register tables. Each client record can relate to many invoices, but each invoice record is for one client. One-to-many relationships like this one prevent repetitious data entry.

You cannot create a *many-to-many* relationship in Access. However, sometimes this type of relationship is useful. For example, suppose you record the time that each employee bills to a client as part of the records in the Invoice table. Each invoice has several employees listed, and each client can have several invoices. You can redesign your tables using an intermediary table called a *junction* table. The junction table has a one-to-many relationship between the other two tables.

Why do I see tables starting with "MSys" in my Database window?

The tables that you see are system tables, which Access uses and maintains in the general operation of the program. Don't modify or delete these tables, because they are very important to the proper operation of Access. By default, these tables are hidden. To hide them again:

1. Choose <u>O</u>ptions from the <u>V</u>iew menu.

2. Select General in the <u>C</u>ategory list box.

3. Move to the Show System Objects item and set the value to No.

4. Select OK to return to your database.

Can I sort the records in my table without having to create a query?

Access provides two ways to sort the records in your table without a query. You can either use the sorting toolbar buttons, or create a filter that sorts the records in the datasheet.

When you sort using the toolbar buttons, you have to select the fields you want to use in sorting the records. In Datasheet view, you can select multiple fields for sorting. The first selected field sorts all records. The second field selected sorts only the records with the same first field value. In a form, you can only sort on a single field. Select the field or fields you want to sort by, and then select the Sort Ascending or Sort Descending button shown here:

Sort Ascending ——— [A↓Z Z↓A] ——— Sort Descending

Tech Note: An ascending sort is A to Z or 1 to 9. A descending sort is Z to A, or 9 to 1.

Access sorts your records. These two buttons are equivalent to choosing Quick Sort from the Records menu and then selecting Ascending or Descending.

Tech Tip: Return the records to their unsorted order by choosing Show All Records in the Records menu, or click the Show All Records toolbar button shown here:

The second way to sort a table is to use filters. Filters can sort using multiple fields. They are somewhat like queries, because you use a QBE grid to define how to sort the records. However, filters do not have all the features that queries do and cannot be saved.

To use a filter to create a complex sort, click the Edit Filter/Sort toolbar button, or choose Edit Filter/Sort from the Records menu to open the Filter window, shown here:

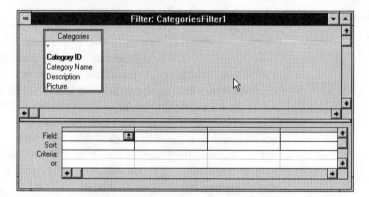

The top half of the Filter window contains the field list for the table. The bottom half contains the QBE grid that creates the sort order or filtering criteria.

Drag each field that you want to the final record order to the Field row of the QBE grid. The first field to sort by appears in the first column, the second in the second, and so on. After adding each field, move to the Sort row directly beneath it. Enter either **Ascending** or **Descending** to set how that field is sorted. You can use both ascending and descending sort orders on different fields in the same filter.

When you finish creating the filter, select the Apply Filter/Sort toolbar button, shown here, or select Apply Filter/Sort from the Records menu. Access applies the filter to the table. After viewing your records in the sorted order, you can remove the filter and return to the default sequence. Just choose Show All Records from the Records menu, or click the Show All Records toolbar button.

Tech Tip: A quick sort creates or adds to the filter. If you open a Filter window after a quick sort, you will see entries in the Sort row of the QBE grid. These are the settings applied by the quick sort.

How can I find all of my overdue accounts?

To find all of your overdue accounts, add a filter that compares the due date in the table with today's date. The filter's criterion is **<Date()**, entered under the Due Date field. This filter shows only the records where the due date precedes today's date. If the table has a field with the date of the bill, then you need to add or subtract days from the Date() function result. For example, if the table has an Invoice Date field and the invoices should be paid by 30 days afterward, the QBE grid in the filter will look like this:

This filters the table to show only the records where the Invoice Date field's date is 30 days before today's date.

Can I change the font used to display my table in Datasheet view?

Yes, you can easily change the font and its size used to display your table in Datasheet view. You can make the change for a single table or change the default font used by all datasheets that do not have their own font setting. Open the table and select Font from the Format menu. In this dialog box, select the font, font size, and font style you want used to display your table.

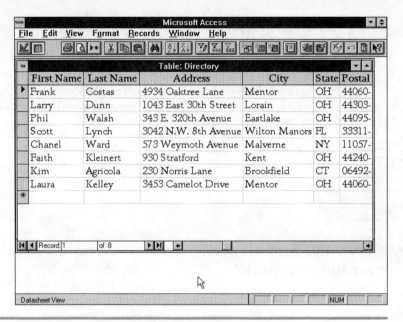

FIGURE 4-1   Change the font size to make tables easier to read

After making your selections, choose OK to close the Font dialog
box. If you enlarge your font to make your table easier to read,
your table might look like Figure 4-1.

You can also set the default font used by all tables and queries
in Datasheet view. To do this, choose Options from the View
menu. Select Datasheet from the Category list box. Now choose
the font name, font size, and various font attributes, including
italics. After setting the options, select OK. The options you select
become the defaults for all tables and queries in Datasheet view,
unless you use the Font command from the Format menu to
change the settings for a specific datasheet.

Why do I get the message "Field *'field name'* can't contain a null value" when I try to save a record?

You are attempting to leave a field blank when its Required
property is set to Yes. A field with the Required property set to
Yes must have an entry, or Access won't let you save the record.
To avoid this error message, either make an entry or change the
field's properties so the field does not require an entry.

Can I combine two similar tables?

Yes, combining two tables is easy with an append query. You may need to combine two similar tables when you receive a database from another user who has been maintaining similar information. For example, when two divisions of your company combine sales departments, you might need to combine the two client list tables into one.

Tech Tip: Queries are database objects that work with the data in tables. See Chapter 5, "Basic Queries," and Chapter 6, "Advanced Queries," for more information on creating and working with queries themselves.

An *append* query takes data from one table and adds it to another table. This query selects all the records you want to combine and includes all of the fields to copy to the other table. When you run this query, Access takes the records selected by the query and adds them to the end of the other table.

The results of the query must match the setup of the table to which you are appending the records. The fields must appear in the same order as in the table and use the same data types. Make sure you check that the query selects the correct records before running it. You can do this by switching to Datasheet view.

Tech Note: A second way to combine tables is with a union query. A union query combines data from several tables, like combining two tables in a one-to-one or one-to-many relationship. The difference is that all data from all tables appears in the final result, even if the record from one table does not have a matching record in the other table. To create a union query, choose SQL Specific from the Query menu and then select Union. Type the SQL statement into the window that performs the union query. You need to be familiar with SQL statements to create this type of query.

Tech Tip: Most of the time when you want data from more than one table combined, you can create a query that creates a dynaset of the data from the tables. A dynaset shows the data selected by a query. It is dynamically connected to the table data that supplies it so that changing the dynaset's data changes the table's data as well. You can use this type of query in forms and reports.

Can I automatically record when a record was last edited?

The only way to record the last time a record was entered or edited is to use a form. You can't do this with the table in Datasheet view, unless you continually reenter the date of the last edit yourself. To have the last date recorded automatically:

1. Open the table in Design view.

2. Add a new Date/Time field called **Last Updated**.

3. Save the table and close it.

4. Open the form you use to edit this table in Design view.

5. Add the Last Updated field to the form as a text box control.

6. Create a new macro with the name **Last Updated Macro** that looks like this:

```
Action:     SetValue
Arguments:  Item:       [Forms]![form name]![Last Updated]
            Expression: Now()
```

7. Save the macro and then close it.

8. Return to the Form window.

9. Choose Select Form from the Edit menu to select the overall form.

10. Choose Properties from the View menu to display the property sheet.

11. Type **Last Updated Macro**, the name of the macro you just created, as the setting for the BeforeUpdate event property of the form.

12. Save and close the form.

Whenever you edit or add a record by using this form, it stores the current date and time in the Last Updated field. If you edit or add new records to the table by using another form or the table's Datasheet view, this field is not automatically updated.

Tech Tip: If you want to document when a record is initially added to a table, add a field and set its DefaultValue property to Now(). Then every time you add a record, Access will add the current time and date to the field with this property.

How can I eliminate duplicate records in my table?

You cannot directly delete duplicate records from a table using Access' features. However, you can create a new table without the duplicate records, and then delete the old table and give the new table its name. To do this:

1. Create a make-table query based on only this table. Make sure that all the fields in the table are included in the QBE grid.

2. Open the query's property sheet by choosing Query Properties from the View menu.

3. Set the Unique Values property to Yes.

4. Run the make-table query. This query selects all the records that have unique values and creates a new table. There are no duplicate records in the new table. You can now delete the old table, and give this new table its name.

Tech Terror: Make sure that you include all of the fields from the table in the QBE grid and display them. Otherwise, your new table might not have all the same fields as your original table.

Can I clear all the records from a table?

Presumably, you want to create a new copy of your table without any data in it. The easiest way is to create a copy containing only the structure of your table. To do this:

1. Select the table you want to copy in the Database window.

2. Choose <u>C</u>opy from the <u>E</u>dit menu.

3. Choose <u>P</u>aste from the <u>E</u>dit menu.

4. Enter the name for the new table in the Table <u>N</u>ame text box.

5. Select the <u>S</u>tructure Only option button and OK.

The table you create has all the same attributes and settings as the original table, but contains none of the data.

Tech Tip: If you want a Counter field in the new table to start with the next sequential number, rather than 1, you should create a delete query that deletes all of the records from the table, instead of creating a new table.

When should I create indexes?

Indexes can speed up Access when working with tables. As a rule of thumb, you want to index any field you use frequently to search, sort, or join the table. However, be careful not to go overboard when creating indexes. Each index you create causes Access to run slightly slower. Too many indexes can slow performance to an unacceptable level and make the database file much larger.

How can I update the records in my table with the values from another table?

If the updated table is simply an updated version of the table in your database, you might delete your old table and give the imported table its name. However, you may find that the imported table only contains data for some of your fields, and that you need to use an update query.

For example, suppose your company just installed a new phone system, so that all of your employees have new phone numbers. The department in charge of installing the phone system just sent you an Access table containing Employee IDs and the new phone numbers assigned to each employee. You don't want to delete your old Employee table, which contains additional data such as benefits, home addresses and phone numbers, and payroll data. To update only the field containing the employee's work phone numbers do this:

1. Create a new query, adding both the original table and the table with the new phone numbers.

2. Create a join between the tables using the primary key, which should be the Employee ID field.

3. Add the fields you want to update from the original table, in this case the Work Number field from the Employee table, to the QBE grid.

4. Make this query an update query by choosing <u>U</u>pdate from the <u>Q</u>uery menu, or by clicking the Update Query toolbar button, shown here:

5. In the Update To row of the QBE grid under each field you want to update, enter the name of the table, a period, and the field from the table with the new data you want to use to update the original table. For example, to update the work phone numbers of your employees, enter the following in the Update To row in the column below the field from the original table that the query will update.

```
[New Numbers].[Numbers]
```

6. Run your update query.

I can't save a table since I added a function as a field's default value. Why?

In Access 2.0, you can use some but not all functions for the DefaultValue property in a table's design. In Access 2.0, Microsoft removed the ability to call some functions from the DefaultValue property. This is done to make Access 2.0 more compatible with language products such as Visual Basic. These products cannot understand Access' custom functions when they are default values in tables. You can see which functions are available by clicking the Build button at the end of the DefaultValue property. You may notice that only Built-In Functions are available under Functions, and that the function categories and the list of functions are much shorter than at other times when you open the Expression Builder.

Tech Tip: The types of functions you cannot use in the DefaultValue property include user-defined functions, functions with references to controls, domain functions, totaling functions, and the CurrentUser() and Eval() functions.

There is still a way to use this function as the default value for the field. Create a form for entering data into the table. Then use the function as the DefaultValue property setting of the control for this field. The DefaultValue property for the control in the form can use all of Access' functions as well as any functions you create with your own Access Basic procedures. It can work in place of the DefaultValue property for the field that is saved as part of the table's design. For an example of how this might work, see the question earlier in this chapter, "Can I automatically record when a record was last edited?," which discusses using the Now() function as the default entry for the Last Updated field.

Tech Tip: The same limit of which functions you can use in the DefaultValue property also applies to the ValidationRule property. Controls for fields in forms have a ValidationRule property. You can add the functions to this property in a form that you cannot add to the field in the table design.

How do I enter the value of a field in the previous record to a new record?

You may find that you use the same entry over and over again in one field of your table. For example, if your employees live in one state, you don't want to enter the state in each record of the Employee table. To copy the entry made for the same field

in the previous record, just press CTRL+' (apostrophe). Access copies the same field's entry from the previous record to the new record.

Tech Tip: When the same entry is used most of the time, add that entry as the field's DefaultValue property.

What is a relationship?

In Access, a *relationship* is a link between two tables that indicates how the data in those tables is related. When you create a relationship, you tell Access which fields in the two tables contain the same data. For example, you might create a relationship between your Employee table and your Payroll table using the Employee ID field in each table. Usually, one of the fields used to create the relationship is the primary key for its table. Both fields must have the same data type. You could not create a relationship using a Number field in one table, and using a Text field in the second table because they contain different types of data.

Tech Tip: When you create a relationship between two tables using a Counter field, one field must be a Long Integer Number field.

To create a relationship between two tables:

1. Choose <u>R</u>elationship from the <u>E</u>dit menu, opening the Relationships window.

If you have not defined relationships before, the Add Table dialog box appears as well. If you have created relationships, but want to add new tables to the window, click the Add Table toolbar button, shown here.

2. Select the tables you want to relate from the <u>T</u>able/Query list box in the Add Table dialog box and select <u>A</u>dd. When you finish adding tables, select <u>C</u>lose.

3. In the Relationships window, drag a field from one table to the related field in another table. Access reminds you which field is the primary key by boldfacing it. For example, to relate the Employee and the Payroll tables, you can drag the Employee ID field from the Payroll table to the Employee table. The Relationships dialog box, shown here, appears.

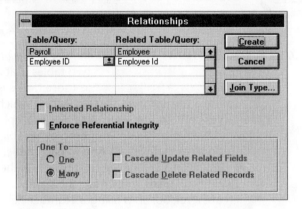

4. Check that the fields being used to create the relationship are given correctly.

5. Select the Enforce Referential Integrity check box to maintain the relationship between the tables. When you enforce referential integrity, Access keeps you from entering records that don't fit the type of relationship between the tables.

6. Select the One or Many option button to decide the type of relationship.

7. Select Create to create the relationship. Relationships are shown in the Relationships window using lines, as you can see in Figure 4-2.

Tech Tip: The type of relationship between the tables is shown by the characters at either end of the join lines. The 1 appears on the "one" side of the relationship. The ∞ (infinity symbol) indicates the "many" side of the relationship.

The tables can have a one-to-one relationship or a one-to-many relationship. In a one-to-one relationship, each record in table A

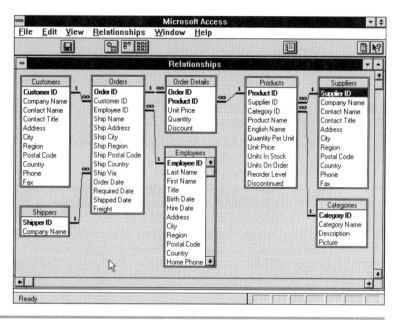

FIGURE 4-2   Join lines indicate relationships in the Relationships window

(the primary table) matches exactly one record in table B (the related table) and vice versa. Therefore, you cannot enter a record in table B unless the related record is already entered in table A and unless no other record in table B is related to the record in table A. In most cases, you want to redesign your tables to combine the information in the two tables. However, sometimes, the one-to-one relationship is intentional.

A one-to-many relationship is where each record in table A (the primary table) matches many records in table B (the related table), but each record in table B relates to only one in table A. Therefore, you can only enter records in table B, the related table, when the related record is already in table A. Unlike a one-to-one relationship, you can add records in table B when table B already has records that are related to the same record in table A. For example, you might have one record in your Employees table with many related records in your Projects table.

Can I print a diagram of the relationships in my database?

Yes, you can print the relationships between your tables.

1. Choose <u>R</u>elationships from the <u>E</u>dit menu.

2. Choose Print De<u>f</u>inition from the <u>F</u>ile menu.

3. Select the Print toolbar button to print this report, which gives a detailed explanation of the relationships in the database.

Tech Note: A laser printer is optimal for printing this graphical image.

To get a quick overview of your relationships, you can capture the Relationships window as a bitmap image, by displaying the window and pressing PRINT SCREEN. Then paste the Clipboard contents into Paintbrush or Word, which can import bitmap images, and print it.

How do I delete a relationship?

You can delete a relationship in Access 2.0 very easily. To delete a relationship:

1. Choose <u>R</u>elationships from the <u>E</u>dit menu to open the Relationships window.

2. Select the line between the tables that indicates the relationships.

3. Press DEL.

4. Select OK when Access prompts you to confirm that you want to delete the relationship.

How can I create a relationship when one field is a Counter field?

As a rule, the fields you use to create a relationship must be the same type. However, if you are trying to create a relationship using a Counter type field, the second field must be a Number type field with the FieldSize property set to Long Integer.

Can I remove some tables from my Relationships window?

Yes, you can remove the tables from your Relationships window without deleting the tables themselves from your database. Just select the table in the Relationships window, and choose Remove Table from the Relationships menu. You can also right-click the table's title bar and select Remove Table. Access removes the table from the Relationships window. Removing the table does not change the relationships the table has. You can always add the table again later using the Add Table dialog box by choosing Add Table in the Relationships menu, or by clicking the Add Table button.

What are cascading updates and deletes?

Cascading updates and deletes are a new feature in Access 2.0. They affect what Access does with data when you update or delete a record in one table that relates to records in other tables. If you have a cascading update, all records in related tables are updated when you change data in a primary table. For example, if you change a customer number in the Customer table, all related tables that contain the customer number update their records to use the new customer number. With a cascading delete, when you delete a record in a primary table, all related data is deleted. This means that when you delete a customer in your Customer table, Access deletes all records for that customer in related tables.

Cascading updates and deletes can be useful, because they can speed data entry and make sure that all related records are updated at the same time. On the other hand, they can also change or delete data without your realizing it. Cascading updates and deletes are not set automatically. You have the opportunity to create them as you create the relationships. In the Relationships dialog box, after you select the Enforce Referential Integrity check box, the dialog box expands to show you some further options. You can then select the Cascade Update Related Fields and Cascade Delete Related Records check boxes before selecting Create to create the relationship. Unless you select one of these check boxes, you don't have cascading updates or deletes.

How can I split a full name field into title, first name, and last name fields?

One way you can split a full name field into its components is with a query. For example purposes, assume that the field name that you want to split is called Full Name. When you create a query, it will have three calculated fields. The entries to appear in the Field row of the QBE grid include

```
Title: Left([Full Name],InStr([Full Name]," "))

First Name: Mid([Full Name],InStr([Full Name]," ")+1,
InStr(InStr([Full Name]," ")+1,[Full Name]," ")
-InStr([Full Name]," "))

Last Name: Trim(Right([Full Name],Len([Full
Name])-InStr(InStr([Full Name]," ")+1,[Full Name]," ")))
```

Next, look at the datasheet for the query to see that the formulas are entered correctly. You can then change the query to a make-table query or an append query, depending on your specific situation. You can also change the query to an update query. Before you change the query, you need to add the fields to the table that will hold the parts of the name. Then, change the query from a select query to an update query. Under the field names that hold the parts of the name, enter the same formulas that the calculated fields use. You can even copy the formulas from the calculated fields in the Field row to the Update To row. You can see how these formulas are placed under the field names in this QBE query.

Field:	Title	First Name	Last Name
Update To:	Left([Full Name],InStr([Full Name]," "))	Mid([Full Name],InStr([Full Name]," ")+1,InStr(InStr([Full Name]," ")):	Trim(Right([F
Criteria:			
or:			

Once you have the query designed, run it. The formulas divide the full name into its pieces and use the pieces as the updated values for the fields. After this query runs, the Title field contains entries like Mr., Mrs., and Miss, while the First Name and Last Name fields contain the first and last names. While this example focuses on names, you use similar calculated fields in a query for other fields that you want to divide.

Tech Tip: Perform a select query before changing the query type to another type of query. By looking at the results of the select query you can make sure that any calculations are entered correctly. You can also see that any criteria select only the records you want.

Can I break up an address field so the address number and the street name are in two fields?

Yes, you can. In the previous question, you saw how you can create a query that shows calculated fields containing parts of a field. You can apply this same type of query to the address. The formulas you will probably use are

```
Address Number: Left([Address],InStr([Address]," "))
Street Name: Trim(Right([Address],Len([Address])
-InStr([Address]," ")))
```

The previous question also described how you can change the select query with these calculated fields into an update query. The update query can enter the formula results as entries for the fields that you have added to the table for the address number and street name.

Basic Queries

A query, in its most basic form, is just a question you ask of an Access table. Access processes the query and displays the records that answer your question in a temporary table called a *dynaset*. With queries, you can answer questions such as which customers have overdue bills or what are your best-selling products.

Queries in Access can serve many functions beyond just answering your questions. Even basic queries can involve a complicated set of criteria that selects the records to display. You can choose which fields of data to display in the answer. You can even combine data from multiple tables in a query's response.

This chapter answers questions about queries in general and the basic select query, which responds to your questions. Advanced queries can also add or update data in a table or even delete outdated records. Chapter 6, "Advanced Queries," can answer your questions about these advanced query types.

FRUSTRATION BUSTERS!

Access uses *QBE* (Query By Example) to simplify query creation. You fill in the empty grid shown in Figure 5-1 to define your question. The different criteria and options on this grid interact to select and sort records. You will want to know what each line on this grid offers. The lines on the grid include

- *Field row*—Contains the names of the fields. If a field is calculated, this cell contains the expression used to calculate the field. The cells beneath this entry relate to this field.

- *Sort row*—Sets whether the field sorts the records in the dynaset.

- *Show row*—Sets whether the field appears in the dynaset.

- *Criteria rows*—Contain the criteria that select which records appear in the dynaset.

FIGURE 5-1   The QBE grid

What is a dynaset?

A *dynaset* is a temporary table created by a query. It is the set of records that answers the question that the query proposes. You can change the data in the dynaset, and Access updates the records in the tables from which the data came. You can even add to tables by entering new records in a dynaset. Likewise, if you change the data in the tables that provide the records in the dynaset, the dynaset changes.

What does QBE stand for?

QBE stands for Query By Example. The name refers to the way you provide examples for the question you want the query to answer. When you open a new query in Design view, you see a Query window, as shown in Figure 5-1. The top half of the window displays the field lists for the tables that are in the query. The bottom half is the QBE grid. You can drag the fields you want in the query from the field lists to the QBE grid's Field row. In the Criteria rows, you can enter examples that you want the query's dynaset to contain. Using QBE allows you to extract the information you want without programming.

Access converts the query design in the QBE grid into an SQL (Structured Query Language) statement. SQL is a standard language used by many database management applications. You can use SQL statements in other Access features to select data. You can create an SQL statement directly, without using the QBE grid. However, unless you are already comfortable using SQL, there's really no good reason to do so.

What is a select query?

Select queries are the most common kind of queries. They simply ask a question of a table or tables, and display the answer to that question. Select queries extract sets of data from your tables. For example, you could create a query to find out which employees worked over 60 hours last week, or which clients have overdue invoices.

When your tables become large, you need to quickly find the data you want. That's what select queries do. Without select queries, your tables are nothing more than long lists of data.

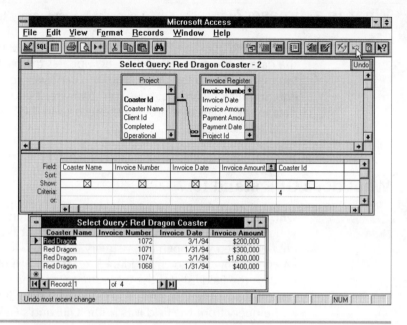

FIGURE 5-2   Select query design and its dynaset

Select queries display dynasets showing temporary tables that display exactly the information you need.

Figure 5-2 shows two copies of a select query. The top copy shows the query's design. You can see that the QBE grid selects which fields appear in the query's dynaset. It selects which records appear by only including the records where the Coaster ID number is 4. The query's dynaset, which you can see in the bottom of Figure 5-2, shows these records.

Tech Tip: Switch to the dynaset from a Query window by clicking the Datasheet View toolbar button, shown here, or by choosing Datasheet from the View menu. This Datasheet View toolbar button and the Design View one are just like the ones you use to switch between Datasheet and Design view for a table.

What is an action query?

An *action* query is a query that can change or move data. Action queries actually do something to tables. Access has four types of action queries:

- *Append* queries add selected data to an existing table.
- *Delete* queries remove data that matches the query's criteria from a table or tables.
- *Make-table* queries create new tables by using the data extracted from other tables.
- *Update* queries update the field entries in an existing table.

What is an SQL-specific query?

An *SQL-specific* query is a query that you can't create with the QBE grid. You create it by writing an SQL statement. Access 2.0 can create the following types of SQL-specific queries:

- *Union* queries combine information from many tables into a single table displayed in a datasheet that cannot be updated.
- *Pass-through* queries send information directly to a database server, letting you work with tables outside your database without actually attaching them.
- *Data-definition* queries can either create or delete a table, add a new field to its design, or create or delete an index for the table.

A query can also use an SQL Select statement as a subquery. However, this Select statement is entered within the QBE grid.

Tech Tip: If you want to use an SQL-specific query, search Access' online help for information on SQL and SQL reserved words to get more information.

Can I check which records an action query will affect before the query is run?

You should always check which records an action query will change before running it. Otherwise, you may discover that your criteria are wrong after you delete all the records in a table. To check affected records, switch to Datasheet view while creating the query.

If the query selects the correct records, you can switch back to the query's Design view and then run it. Switch back to the query's design by clicking the Design View toolbar button or by choosing Query Design from the View menu. Run the action query by clicking the Run toolbar button, shown here, or by choosing Run from the Query menu.

How many tables can I use in a query?

You can use up to 32 tables in a query. The fields from the table can either appear in the query's dynaset or select which records from another table appear in the dynaset.

How many fields can I sort by in my query?

You can sort by up to ten fields in your query. To sort by a field in your query, you select Ascending or Descending from the Sort row under the field's name. Access starts sorting by the leftmost field and works its way right.

Tech Tip: Don't be surprised if you add a field more than once to a QBE grid. For example, you may want a field that you are using for sorting to appear in a different column of the query's dynaset. The copy of the field with the selected Show check box is the one that appears in the dynaset.

How many characters can I have in a cell of the QBE grid?

You can have up to 1,024 characters in a cell in the QBE grid. You may need this many characters when you enter complicated expressions for criteria or calculated fields.

How can I see all of a really long criterion in my QBE grid?

Access provides a way to easily view a lengthy entry in your QBE grid. While in the cell, press SHIFT+F2. Access opens the Zoom box, which displays the long entry, as shown here:

Tech Tip: The Zoom box can also display long entries in other parts of a query, such as an entry in a Field row. You can use this Zoom box in other areas of Access, such as when creating controls or entering data in a table.

How can I tell if a query is updatable?

When a query is updatable, you can enter new information in the query to update the underlying table. The easiest way to check if the query can update the underlying table is to check the last record in Datasheet view. If it is a blank record with an asterisk on the selector, then you can update tables using this query.

There are several reasons that a query might not be updatable. Queries that aren't updatable include

- Crosstab, pass-through, or union queries
- Queries that calculate totals
- Queries that include attached tables without indexes or primary keys
- Queries for which permission to update or delete records is not available
- Queries including multiple tables or queries that aren't joined
- Queries with the Unique Values property set to Yes

Some queries let you update some fields in the query, but not others. Fields that cannot be updated include

- Some fields in a query based on tables with a one-to-many relationship
- Calculated fields
- Fields from databases that were opened as read-only or that are on a read-only drive
- Fields deleted or locked by another user
- A Memo or OLE Object field in a *snapshot,* which is an unchanging dynaset created by SQL-specific queries

Tech Tip: Another way to check if a query is updatable is to see if the Allow Editing command on the Records menu is dimmed or not. If it is dimmed, you can't update the records. If it is not dimmed, but doesn't have a check mark in front of it, you have turned off the ability to edit records. You need to select this command again to turn it back on.

How do I turn on the Rushmore query technology so my queries can take advantage of it?

You don't have to because it is already on! Access automatically uses the Rushmore technology. The Rushmore technology optimizes your queries when the criteria use certain types of expressions. Since Access does this behind the scenes, you don't need to do anything. If you are curious about this new feature, search the online help for Rushmore technology.

Tech Note: Access tries not to use Rushmore technology if your query contains ODBC data sources. Also, Paradox and Btrieve tables cannot use this technology. However, Rushmore is always used with Access tables.

Can I get a query to return a specified number of the highest or lowest values in a field?

With Access 2.0 you can! Access 2.0 queries include a new TopValues property. You can use this property to create a query that returns a set number of the highest or lowest values in a field. For example, you can create a query that returns the records of your top five salespeople. To do this:

1. Create the query to select which records you want included.

2. Sort the query by the field from which you want to select the top or bottom records. If you want to select the largest values in that field, sort it in descending order. To select the lowest values, sort the field in ascending order.

3. Open the Query Properties sheet by clicking the Properties toolbar button or by selecting Properties from the View menu. If you see Field Properties at the top of the window, click an empty area of the query design.

4. Type the number or percentage of records you want to display in the TopValues property. For example, enter **5** to have the query return the top five values or **10%** to have the query return the top 10% of the values.

5. Click the Datasheet View toolbar or choose Datasheet from the View menu to display the query's dynaset.

Can I use a query to find duplicate values in a table?

The easiest way to locate duplicate values in a table is to use the Find Duplicates Query Wizard, a new feature in Access 2.0. This Wizard prompts you for information about how you want to search for duplicates and then creates the query based on your answers. The Wizard has four steps:

1. Select the table in which you want to find duplicate records.

2. Select the fields you want to search for duplicates. The query will count as duplicates any records that are the same in all of the fields you select here, even if they are different in other fields.

3. Select any other fields you want displayed in the query's dynaset. These fields won't be checked for duplicates.

4. Enter a name for the query, and choose whether you want to open it in Datasheet or Design view.

If you look at the query's design, you will see a Select statement like the one shown here. This Select statement is an SQL statement that is a subquery to the query the Wizard created.

```
┌─────────────────────────────────────────────────────────────┐
│ □          Select Query: Order Details Extended        ▼ │▲│ │
├─────────────────────────────────────────────────────────┼─┤ │
│ SELECT DISTINCTROW [Order Details].[Order ID], Products.[Product Name], [Order │▲│
│ Details].[Product ID], [Order Details].[Unit Price], [Order Details].Quantity, [Order │
│ Details].Discount, CLng([Order Details].[Unit Price]*[Quantity]*[1- │
│ [Discount]]*100)/100 AS [Extended Price] │
│ FROM Products INNER JOIN [Order Details] ON Products.[Product ID] = [Order │
│ Details].[Product ID]; │
│                                                             │▼│ │
└─────────────────────────────────────────────────────────────┘
```

Tech Tip: Remember, to start the Find Duplicates
Query Wizard, select <u>N</u>ew in the Database window
while viewing queries, click the Query <u>W</u>izards button,
and select Find Duplicates Query.

A calculated field in my query is based on a Number field that has a Scientific Format property. Why does the field use a General format in the query's dynaset?

Access 2.0 supports property inheritance from tables to queries. This means that the properties set for a table field are automatically adopted by that field in a query. Therefore, if your Number field uses the Scientific format in the table, it uses the same format in the query.

The problem is that the calculated field is not the same as your Number field. Calculated fields do not inherit properties from the fields used in the field's expression. After all, suppose you used two different fields in the calculated field's expression, each of which used a different format. How would Access know which format to use?

To format your calculated field in the query, you need to set its Format property directly. To change this property, move to the calculated field in the QBE grid. Click the Properties toolbar button, or choose <u>P</u>roperties from the <u>V</u>iew menu. Move to the Format property and select Scientific from the drop-down list.

My query includes a calculated field that subtracts two Date/Time fields. However, the calculated field displays fractional numbers instead of times. How do I see the times?

The fractional number that you see in the field is the date/time serial number. Access stores the dates and times you enter as date/time serial numbers that it can use in calculations. The integer part of the number indicates the number of days between the two dates you have entered. The decimal fraction part indicates the portion of the day that passed between the two times entered. The best way to see the times these numbers represent is to create an Access Basic Function procedure that extracts the correct elapsed time. This Function procedure creates a string out of the time information stored as a fraction. To create this procedure:

1. Select the Module button in the Database window.

2. Select New.

3. Type the following code into the Module window:

```
Function HrsMinsSecs (TimeVar As Double)
Dim Hrs As Long, Mins As String, Secs As String
If IsNull(TimeVar) Then
    HrsMinsSecs = Null
Else
    Mins = Format(DatePart("n", TimeVar), "00")
    Secs = Format(DatePart("s", TimeVar), "00")
    Hrs = (Fix(TimeVar) * 24) + DatePart("h", TimeVar)
    HrsMinsSecs = Hrs & ":" & Mins & ":" & Secs
End If
End Function
```

4. Move to the Field cell for the calculated cell and enter

```
=HrsMinsSecs(Value To Convert)
```

For this example, you might enter
=HrsMinsSecs([Last Date]-[First Date]).

5. Click the Datasheet View button to display the query's
dynaset. The calculated field should now display as a time
with the HH:NN:SS format. For example, if Last Date equals
12/25/94 22:30 and First Date equals 12/24/94 18:00,
this Function procedure displays the result as 28:30:00
instead of 1.1875.

Tech Tip: You can also change the field's Format property to display its
value as a time. However, the Format property can give an incorrect
value if the elapsed time is over 24 hours. Therefore, this function,
while more complicated, is a more dependable solution.

After I deleted the Format property settings for a field in my query, it still used the same format, instead of the one assigned in the table. What can I do?

If your dynaset does not display
using the current property settings,
something has happened to prevent
Access from updating the display. To
force Access to update the display, save
the query and close it. When you open
the query and run it again, the field
will revert to the formatting applied
to it in the table.

My query's calculated field displays too many places to the right of the decimal. Can I limit the places it shows?

Yes, you can control how many decimal places the field shows.
To limit the decimal places:

1. Click the Design View toolbar button, or choose Query
Design in the View menu to switch back to the query's
Design view.

2. Move to the calculated field whose decimal places you
want to limit.

3. Choose Properties from the View menu, or click the
Properties toolbar button.

4. Move to the Format property.

5. Select one of the formats from the drop-down list.

6. Move to the Decimal Places property.

7. Enter the number of decimal places you want.

8. Click the Datasheet View toolbar button, or choose Datasheet in the View menu to return to the datasheet. You can see only the selected number of digits after the decimal point.

I created a calculated field that divides two numbers, but the results don't show any decimal places, though they should. What's wrong?

There are two reasons why your calculated field may not show any digits to the right of the decimal place: using the wrong operator or using the DecimalPlaces property setting.

To find the cause of this problem, switch back to the query's Design view. Double-check that you used / (slash) as the division operator in the formula, instead of \ (backslash). The \ (backslash) is for integer division. It divides two integers and returns an integer result. If the values you divide with a backslash have decimal fractions, Access rounds them to perform this calculation. Therefore, 234.56\21.34 is the same as 235\21. If this is the cause of your problem, simply change your \ (backslash) to a / (slash), and your formula should now work correctly.

If the problem isn't an incorrect operator, perhaps you have set the DecimalPlaces property to 0. To check this, move to the field and choose Properties from the View menu. If the DecimalPlaces property is set to 0, clear the entry or set it to the number of decimal places that you want.

When I try to run my query, I get a message saying "Can't group on fields selected with '*'." What can I do?

Some of the reasons you might get this message include

■ The OutputAllFields property is set to Yes. You will need to go into the properties for the queries and make sure that the OutputAllFields property is set to No.

- The QBE grid for a crosstab query includes a * in the Field row. Remove the * from the QBE grid.

- You tried to make the select query a crosstab query, and the QBE grid already has a * in the Field row. Remove the * before you change the query into a crosstab query.

- You are trying to execute an SQL statement that has an aggregate function or Group By clause as well as an *. Change the SQL statement to remove the asterisk, aggregate function, or Group By clause.

Can I combine the criteria in my query with a logical And or Or?

Access automatically combines the criteria you enter in the QBE grid with logical Ands and Ors depending on where you enter them. You'll need to know how Access does this to make sure that you enter criteria in such a way that you get the desired results.

Logical Ands combine the criteria so that records need to match both criteria to be included in the dynaset. Access combines all criteria in the same row using the logical And. Therefore, records must match all of the criteria on a single row before they are included in the query's dynaset. You can apply two criteria to the same field and combine them with a logical And, as in >50000 And <500000.

Logical Ors combine the criteria, requiring records to match either one of the criteria to be included in the dynaset. Access uses the logical Or to combine criteria on different rows in the QBE grid. Therefore, if you enter two criteria for a single field, one below the other, the records need to satisfy either one of the two criteria to be included in the query's dynaset.

One way to visualize a logical Or is to consider the criteria rows as different lanes in a race, as shown in Figure 5-3. Each row is a single lane, while each criterion is a hurdle. To be included in the query's dynaset, a record must finish racing through one of these lanes without failing to pass a hurdle. If it fails a hurdle in one lane, which means failing to match a criterion, it can try the other lanes or rows. If it cannot finish any one lane, it drops out of the race and is not included in the dynaset. If it can pass any one of the lanes, it is included in the dynaset. A logical And, on the other hand, is like the second track that has two hurdles to pass.

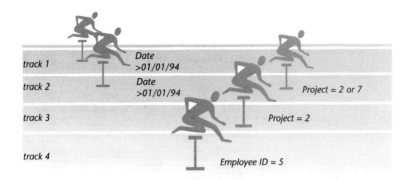

track 1	Date >01/01/94
track 2	Date >01/01/94
	Project = 2 or 7
track 3	Project = 2
track 4	
	Employee ID = 5

FIGURE 5-3   Diagram of how the different rows of criteria work

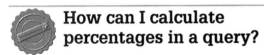

How can I calculate percentages in a query?

You can calculate percentages using the DCount function to calculate the total that the percentage field uses in its expression. The steps can be involved, so you will want to see this in action. The following example shows how to calculate percentages in a query. It calculates the percentage of products that belong to each category using the Products table in the Northwind sample database provided with Access 2.0. To create this query:

1. Create a new query and include only the Products table in it.

2. Click the Totals button, the one with a Σ character on it. This inserts the Total row into the QBE grid. In this row, you can select the totaling action you want to perform on the field.

3. Add the Category ID field from the Products table to the QBE grid. You can drag it from the field list, double-click it in the field list, or select it from the Field row's drop-down list box. Its Total row entry automatically defaults to "Group By."

4. Add the Product ID field to the QBE grid and change its Total row entry to Count.

5. Rename the Product ID field. Click Product ID until you see the insertion point instead of having the entire field selected. Move to the beginning of the field and type **Products Per Category:**, making sure to include the colon. You want this field to have a different name, since you will later be referring to it for the total number of products in each category, and you cannot use Product ID. The query design will look like this:

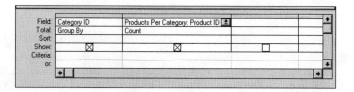

If you run the query now, you will see that it returns the results shown in the following illustration, which is a count of products per category. You will also notice that the Products field is renamed.

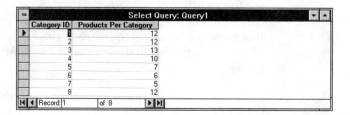

6. Type the following expression in the Field row cell for the next empty column:

```
Total Number of Products: DCount("[Product Id]","Products")
```

This will return the total number of records in the Products table. The Group By in the Total row will have no effect. Usually DCount has three arguments, but since the last one is not supplied, this function includes all the table's records in the calculation.

7. Type the following expression in the Field row cell for the next column:

```
Percentage: [Products Per Category] / [Total Number of Products]
```

This expression returns a decimal value that represents the percentage. The query can display this value as a percentage by changing the Format property.

8. Choose Properties from the View menu, or click the Properties toolbar button to display the property sheet if you do not see it already.

9. Select the Percentage calculated field in the QBE grid and select Percent for the Format property in the property sheet.

10. Change the Total row entries for both the third and fourth fields to "Expression" and run the query. Your query's design looks like this:

Field:	Category ID	Products Per Category:	Total Number of Products:	Percentage: ±	
Total:	Group By	Count	Expression	Expression	
Sort:					
Show:	☒	☒	☒	☒	☐
Criteria:					
or:					

Note that you could combine the third and fourth fields into a single calculation and omit the third field altogether, by entering the following in the Percentage field name:

```
Percentage: [Products Per Category]/DCount("[Product Id]","Products")
```

Can my query extract just the day, month, or year from a Date field?

Yes, if you want to display just the day, month, or year from a field, create a custom format that displays the one element you want. Table 5-1 shows several custom formats you can use to do this, and the results of applying that format to the date

Format	Returns
DD	08
DDD	Sun
DDDD	Sunday
MM	12
MMM	Dec
MMMM	December
YY	96
YYYY	1996

TABLE 5-1   Custom formats for limiting dates

December 8, 1996. To apply a custom date format, move to the field in Design view, choose <u>P</u>roperties from the <u>V</u>iew menu, and move to the Format property. Enter the format, as shown in the table. The next time you run the query, you will see the new formats.

Tech Tip: You can also use these custom formats as the Format property setting for report and form controls.

If you really do want a calculated field to equal one part of a date the field's expression can use one of Access' many built-in functions. These functions that return a part of a date or time are listed in Table 5-2. As an example, a query that uses these functions appears in the following illustration. The first calculated field contains Year: Year([Invoice Date]) and the second field contains Month: Month([Invoice Date]).

Year	Month	Last Name	First Name	TotalSales
1995	7	Kleinert	Faith	$68,023.00
1995	5	Walsh	Phil	$45,693.00
1995	5	Lynch	Scott	$21,309.00
1995	6	Ward	Larry	$58,930.00
1995	6	Agricola	Kim	$19,480.00
1995	6	Ward	Chanel	$48,930.00
				$0.00

Select Query: Query1

Record: 7   of 7

Function	Returns
Day(*date*)	The day of the month number
Month(*date*)	The month of the year number
Year(*date*)	The year
Weekday(*date*)	The day of the week number
Hour(*time*)	The hour
Minute(*time*)	The number of minutes
Second(*time*)	The number of seconds

TABLE 5-2   Built-in functions that return part of a date

Can my query select records based on one word in a Memo or Text field?

Yes, you can have your query search for a single word in a longer entry. For example, to search for the word "Blue" in a field, open the query in Design view. Move to the Criteria row beneath the field and enter **Like "*" & "Blue" & "*"**. Run the query by clicking the Datasheet View button, or by choosing Data_sheet from the _V_iew menu.

How can I find all the records in a table that were entered this month?

Assuming that the table has a field containing the date that records have been entered, you can create a query that chooses only the records you entered this month. To do this, create your query as normal. Then, assuming the field that contains the date of entry is named Entry Date, enter **Month([Entry Date])** in the Field row to create a calculated field. The Month function extracts just the month from your Date field. Move to the Criteria row for this column and enter **Month(Date())**. This expression extracts the month of the current date. When you run this query, the dynaset shows only the records entered during the current month.

Can I use an Access Basic variable as a criterion in a query?

The only way to refer to an Access Basic variable is by using Access Basic code. Therefore, if you want to use an Access Basic variable as a criterion in your query, you first need to create a function that equals the value of that variable. Your function would look like:

```
Function GetValue()          'Function to get a value of a variable
GetValue = Variable Name     'Sets GetValue function equal to a
                              globally declared variable

End Function                 'End of function
```

You can then enter the function's name as the criterion.

How can I shorten the results of a calculation from four decimal places to two, so I can use the rounded results in another expression?

If you just needed to control how many decimal places appear in the Datasheet view, you could change the Decimal Places property. However, since you want to use the calculation again later, you need to control the actual number. To do this, combine the Val and Format functions. For example, enter

```
Val(Format(expression,"#.00"))
```

The Format property extracts the number by using only two decimal places. However, in the process, the Format property converts the number into text. The Val function converts the text back into a number.

I just opened a query and its QBE grid has changed. Is something wrong with my query?

Nothing is wrong with your query. Access sometimes rearranges your QBE grid as it optimizes it. These changes can include dividing criteria into smaller pieces and rearranging the fields. Your query selects the same data; it just has a different appearance. You won't see these changes until you close a Query window and then reopen it.

Why do I get rounding errors when I create a calculated field by using fields with the Currency format?

The calculated field is not inheriting the Format property of the table field. Therefore, the results of the calculated field often round improperly. You can correct this by changing the calculation you are using. These steps assume that you want to round to two decimal places.

What you need to do is multiply the result of your calculated field by 100. For example, if you multiply 1.2349 by 100, the result is 123.49. Then you use the Int function that truncates the number, removing the decimal places, resulting in 123. Then you divide this number by 100 again, giving you 1.23, the correctly shortened result. Use the CCur() function on this number to convert it back to a currency number.

In doing this, you are nesting the formula for the calculated field within another formula. To make the final formula easier to read, you may want to create two calculated fields, your original one and the one that does this. For example, if your calculated field is called Profits1, the new field's entry might be **Profits: CCur(Int(Profits1*100)/100)**.

Why does my query, which has no criteria, have fewer records in the dynaset than in my table?

If your query is based on more than one table, your join properties may not be set properly. This limits the number of records that appear. To check the join properties, switch back to Design view. Then, double-click each join line connecting the field lists. You can choose from three types of joins. Select the appropriate type and select OK.

Why can't I use * in an IIf function when I want to return the complete field entry when the IIf expression is true?

You can't use the * as a wildcard character to represent the complete contents of the field in the IIf function. This function assumes that * is a literal character when it appears. Therefore, it returns * instead of a field's contents when the expression is true. If you want to return the complete contents of the field, enter the field name as the argument. For example, a calculated field that displays an invoice date when it is before today's date and nothing otherwise might contain the following Field row entry:

```
Date: IIf([Invoice Date]<Date(),[Invoice Date])
```

Advanced Queries

The previous chapter discussed both general questions about queries and basic select queries. This chapter covers Access' more advanced queries, including the new SQL-specific queries.

  Select queries are fairly straightforward because they simply select the records to display in response to a question that you pose. The more advanced queries provide new options and new challenges. The following Frustration Busters box explains what each type of advanced query does.

FRUSTRATION BUSTERS!

Access provides a wide variety of queries. Figuring what each type of query can do for you is often confusing, so here is a synopsis of the features of each advanced query:

- *Crosstab query*—Summarizes data in a compact row and column format. You can choose fields that provide row and column headings, then choose which field is summarized in the body of the table.

- *Action queries*—Perform an action using the data they select. Access has four action queries:

  - *Make-table action query*—Creates a new table from the selected data.

  - *Delete action query*—Deletes the selected data from an existing table.

  - *Append action query*—Adds the selected data to an existing table.

  - *Update action query*—Updates the data in an existing table with the selected data.

- *SQL-specific queries*—Can only be created in Access using an SQL statement. Access supports three types of SQL specific queries:

  - *Pass-through SQL-specific query*—Passes commands directly to the ODBC driver.

  - *Union SQL-specific query*—Selects the specified records from two or more tables.

  - *Data definition SQL-specific query*— Creates or edits a table in the current database.

I want my parameter query to select all records when a user doesn't specify parameters. How can I do this?

In parameter queries, users are prompted to supply entries each time you run the query. The entries often provide criteria. This lets you create a query with criteria that change every time. For example, your parameter query could present the invoices for a single week. The dates the user enters determine which week's invoices are included in the dynaset.

To produce a parameter query that displays all records when no criteria are supplied, you need to create a criterion that uses the wildcard character. This query either uses the value provided by the user or matches everything. For example, your criterion in the QBE grid might look like this:

```
Like "*" & [Enter a Value] & "*"
```

If the user does not enter the value to match, then the criterion matches all entries in that field because of the * wildcard character. If the user does enter the value, the criterion matches only those values. The wildcard character is ignored because the value entered is the entire content of the field. When you run the query, you will see a prompt like the one shown next. If you type **Smith**, the query's criterion equals Like "*Smith*". If you do not type anything, the criterion equals Like "**".

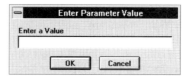

Can I create a parameter query that prompts for a single letter, then returns all records in which the Text field's entry starts with that letter?

Yes, you can create a parameter query that returns all records in which the entries in a Text field start with a single letter provided by the user. You do this by combining the letter entered with the

* wildcard character for that field's criterion. For example, you can make this entry in the QBE grid:

```
Like [Your Parameter] & "*"
```

This criterion matches any entries starting with the letter the user enters.

My query has separate date and time fields, but I want to select records based on a combination of the date and time. How can I do this?

You need to add a calculated field to your query that you use to select records, but which does not display. The query's parameters supply entries for this field. For example, create a calculated field by entering **New Time: [Date Field] & " " & [Time Field]** in the Field row, assuming your date and time fields are named Date Field and Time Field. Next, enter a criterion for this field, including the parameter prompts for where you want the dates and times placed. For example, you can enter **Between [Enter beginning date and time] and [Enter ending date and time]**. If you don't want this field displayed, remember to clear the check box in the Show row of the QBE grid. When the query is run, the query prompts for the beginning and ending dates and times.

Tech Tip: If you are uncertain that the query's user will correctly enter the dates and times. you can have separate parameter prompts. The criterion can join the dates and times as in **Between [Enter beginning date] + [Enter beginning time] and [Enter ending date] + [Enter ending time]**.

I want to create a parameter query in which users only have to enter part of a Text field's entry. Can I do this?

Presumably, you want to create a parameter query in which the user does not have to enter the complete entry to have Access find matches. For example, you can enter part of a name when responding to the prompt for the parameter, but have the query return all records that include your response, even when it's only part of the name. You can do this by concatenating the * wildcard and the parameter value.

For example, suppose you want to find matching entries in your First Name field. You might enter the following criterion in the Criteria row:

```
Like [Enter First Name] & "*" Or Is Null
```

This criterion matches any entries with the complete parameter value or with the complete parameter value and trailing text. For example, if the user enters **Jo** in response to the parameter, Access searches the First Name field and returns all records containing "Jo" or "Jo" combined with other text, such as John, Joan, and Joseph.

Specifying "Or Is Null" allows the user to enter no parameter value and retrieve all records, including ones that have no entry for that field.

Why can't I update my crosstab query?

A crosstab query cannot be updated. A crosstab query produces a *snapshot* instead of a dynaset. A snapshot is a static picture of a set of records. You can edit the data in a dynaset; you cannot edit the data in a snapshot. This is simply a feature of how Access works and cannot be worked around. When you try to edit a crosstab query, the status line displays "This Recordset is not updatable."

Can I create more than one column heading in my crosstab query?

You cannot create a crosstab query with multiple column headings. However, you can have many row headings. Select another row heading by adding the field to the QBE grid and choosing Row Heading in the Crosstab row. As an example, Figure 6-1 shows two versions of the same crosstab query so

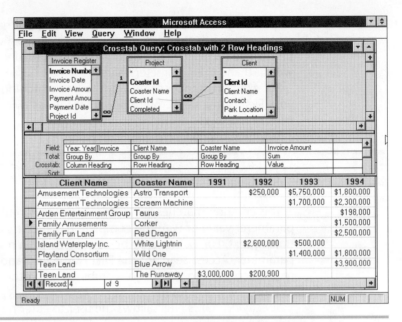

FIGURE 6-1   Crosstab query that uses two row headings and its design

you can see both its design and resulting datasheet. In this query, Client Name and Coaster Name are both row headings. The records in the query are divided by client and then divided for each client by the coaster type.

Tech Tip: The order of fields in the QBE grid decides the order in which Access divides the records into groups. The first field that has Row Heading in the Crosstab row is the first column in the crosstab's datasheet and initially divides the records into groups.

Can I turn my crosstab query into a table?

Yes, you can convert a crosstab query into a table. To do so, create a crosstab query. Then convert it into a make-table query by clicking the Make-Table

Query toolbar button, shown here, or by choosing Make Table from the Query menu. Then you can enter the name of the table in the Table Name text box and select OK. However, the table is not created until you run the query by choosing Run from the Query menu or by clicking the Run toolbar button.

Tech Note: The table you create with a converted crosstab query does not use the same layout as the crosstab query's Datasheet view. Instead, it presents the records as if you had converted the crosstab query into a select query, using the usual datasheet orientation and none of the summarizing available with the crosstab query.

When I press SHIFT+F9 in my crosstab query, it doesn't requery the underlying table to reflect changes. How can I get my crosstab query to display up-to-date information?

Your crosstab query displays a static snapshot of data rather than a dynamic dynaset. It captures the data to show in the crosstab query at the moment when you show the crosstab's datasheet. This means that it does not automatically update when you change the data in the underlying table. The easiest way to display up-to-date information is to close the query and reopen it. If you want to update the query each time you press SHIFT+F9, switch to the Design view of the query. Display the property sheet for the field you are using as the column heading. Make an entry in the Column Heading property. The entries you make for this property are the names of the columns you want displayed. They must precisely match the actual column headings. For example, if the column headings are the years 1990 through 1995, you would enter **1990,1991,1992,1993,1994,1995**. After you switch back to Datasheet view, you will find that you can rerun the query by pressing SHIFT+F9. Adding these column headings makes the query less flexible, but now it can be requeried.

How do I create a pass-through query?

A pass-through query is a query that sends SQL commands directly to an ODBC database server. A pass-through query lets you work with tables on an ODBC database server without attaching the tables to an Access database. A pass-through query can also run procedures stored on the ODBC database server. You can use a pass-through query to change data in the database being edited, to create a database object, or to perform an action similar to an action query. You do this by entering the correct SQL commands for these actions. These actions are done in the ODBC database server, not in Access. Since Access doesn't process the commands in a pass-through query, you need to use the syntax that the server expects when you enter the commands to send to the server. Unless you are acquainted with this syntax from the application's documentation, you should not use a pass-through query.

If you feel comfortable using SQL to work with a table or database, you can create a pass-through query to send commands to work with that data. To create a pass-through query:

1. Select the Query tab in the Database window.

2. Select <u>N</u>ew, then select <u>N</u>ew Query to open a blank new query.

3. Select <u>C</u>lose to avoid adding any field lists to the Query window.

4. Choose S<u>Q</u>L Specific from the <u>Q</u>uery menu; then select <u>P</u>ass-Through.

5. Enter the commands you want to send to the ODBC driver.

6. Open the property sheet for the query by clicking the Properties toolbar button or by choosing <u>P</u>roperties from the <u>V</u>iew menu.

7. Move to the ODBC Connect Str property and specify the information needed to connect to the ODBC database server. You may be able to enter this information by clicking the Build button and making selections.

8. Select Yes for the Return Records property if you want to get information back from this query or No if you just want to execute the commands without returning any information.

9. Choose <u>R</u>un from the <u>Q</u>uery menu or click the Run toolbar button to run the query.

Tech Tip: If the pass-through query returns data, you can run the query by clicking the Datasheet View toolbar button.

Can I update the records returned by a pass-through query?

No, you cannot edit the records returned by a pass-through query in Access, nor can you enter new ones. This data is a snapshot rather than a dynaset.

Are the results of a union query updatable?

No, they are not updatable. A union query returns all of the specified records from one or more tables. These records are considered part of a *snapshot,* which is a static display of data, unlike the dynamic dynaset. If you want a version of the data from a union query that you can edit, you need to save it, and then create a separate make-table action query based on the union query. After you run the make-table action query, you can update the records in the new table.

Tech Tip: If you want a dynaset from several tables that you can edit, create a select query. The only reason you would want a union query rather than a select query is when you want all records in all tables in the query to appear, even if there is no matching record in the other tables.

Can I convert a pass-through query into a make-table query?

No, you cannot. If you convert a pass-through query to any other type of query, it loses its SQL statement. The query no longer produces a result.

Tech Tip: If you want the data from a pass-through query placed in a table, create a separate make-table query that uses the pass-through query as its source of data.

When I try to run a pass-through query, I get a timeout error. What can I do?

By default, Access waits 60 seconds to get a complete response to your pass-through query. If the response is not complete, it returns a timeout error. This is to prevent you from waiting a very long time for the result of the query. If you suspect that your pass-through query will take longer than one minute to run, open the query's property sheet. Move to the ODBC Timeout property and enter a new number of seconds to wait. If you set this property to 0, Access never presents a timeout error.

Do I have to attach the SQL tables I want to work with in a pass-through query?

No, you do not have to attach the tables you want to work with in a pass-through query. This type of query allows you to work with the tables by using their server rather than Access.

Can I add carriage returns to a field name in a make-table query, so the field names in the table have multiple lines?

Field names in a table cannot contain carriage returns. They can never be more than one line. If you try, you will receive several error messages and you cannot run the query.

Can I create a query in Access Basic without saving it as an object in my database?

Yes, you can do this by using the CreateQueryDef method to create the query, and then using the Execute and Close methods to delete it. An example of this code might look like this:

```
Dim TempQuery As QueryDef       ' Assumes MyDB is already
                                  assigned a database object
Set TempQuery = MyDB.CreateQueryDef("", "Update Table1 Set
Table1.Field1 = Field1 * 1.1;")
TempQuery.Execute               ' Statements for working with
                                  the temporary query

TempQuery.Close
```

How can I find the records in one table that do not have related records in a second table?

The easiest way to do this is to use the Find Unmatched Query Wizard. To use this Wizard:

1. Select the Query tab in the Database window.

2. Select New.

3. Select Query Wizards.

4. Select Find Unmatched Query and OK.

5. Select the table containing the records you want returned as not matching the records in a second table, and then select Next.

6. Select the table to which you want to relate the first table, and then select Next.

7. Select the fields that contain the same data to create a join and click the <=> button. Access may have already selected the fields for you based on defined relationships. Then select Next.

8. Select the fields you want to appear in the dynaset and select Next.

9. Select Finish to display the query.

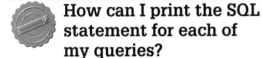

How can I print the SQL statement for each of my queries?

Access converts all of your queries into SQL statements before they are run. To print the SQL statement for each of your queries, you must use the Database Documentor add-in.

1. Choose Add-ins from the File menu while in the Database window.

2. Select Database Documentor.

3. Select Queries from the Object Type drop-down list box.

4. Choose Select All to report on all the queries.

5. Select Options.

6. Clear all the check boxes except SQL and select the Nothing radio button.

7. Select OK twice to create the report. The beginning of this report looks like this:

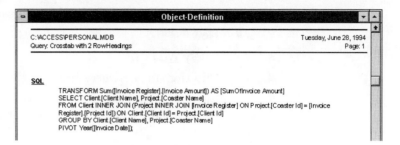

This particular SQL statement belongs to the crosstab query shown in Figure 6-1. Each query's SQL statement is on a separate page.

You can also display the SQL statement in the Query window. Click the SQL toolbar button (the one that shows "SQL") or choose SQL from the View menu. You now see the SQL statement, which is the same as the one just shown, here:

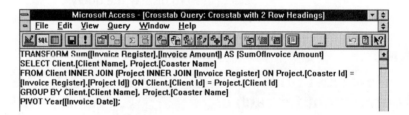

Tech Tip: You can print the SQL statement for a single query by choosing Print Definition from the File menu while highlighting the query in the Database window. You will still want to clear all of the check boxes except SQL and select the Nothing radio button. Select OK once to create the report for the query.

I want to use entries in a form as criteria for the query on which the form is based. How do I do this?

When you enter criteria in a form and then run a query using those criteria you are using a *query by form*. A query by form is created like most parameter queries. The difference is that a parameter query includes the parameter's prompt, while the query has the full reference to the control in the form. For example, the following QBE grid gets the criteria from a form. It contains a full reference to the control in a form.

Field:	Coaster Id		Invoice Number	Invoice Date	Invoice Amount
Sort:					
Show:		☐	☒	☒	☒
Criteria:	[Forms]![Clients and Their Coasters]![Field10]				
or:					

My queries print with a header and a footer. Can I get rid of them?

No, you cannot print your query from Access without including the default header and footer. The header includes the query name and the current date. The footer includes the page number. If you want to print your query's data without these, try one of these options:

- Create an AutoReport for the query or create a report using a Report Wizard. Once you see the preview of the AutoReport, switch to the report's design and change the Visible property for the Report Header, Report Footer, Page Header, and Page Footer sections to No. Then the report prints only the Detail section to show the query's data.

- Transfer the query's data to another application, such as a word processor, and print it there. The easiest way to do this is to select the entire query, copy it to the Clipboard, and then paste it into a word processor such as the Write accessory.

- Choose Output To from the File menu from the query's datasheet or while the query is highlighted in the Database window. Choose Rich Text Format (*.rtf) from the Select Format list box; then select OK. Enter the name for the file and select OK again. You can open this file in another application such as a word processor, and print it without the header and footer.

I want to display my query's dynaset without allowing edits. Can I do this without setting security on the query object?

One way to do this is to create a form that displays the results of your query on a datasheet. To create this form:

1. Highlight the query and click the AutoForm button to quickly create a form that includes all the fields from the query.

2. Switch to the form's design.

3. Display the form's property sheet.

4. Set the ViewsAllowed property to Datasheet.

5. Set the DefaultEditing property to Read Only.

6. Set the AllowEditing property to Unavailable.

Now when you look at the form, you will see a datasheet. You cannot edit the datasheet.

Tech Tip: You can copy the SQL statement from the query and paste it to the form's RecordSource property. Then you can delete the query, and the form still shows the correct data in its datasheet.

Forms

An Access form shows and lets you enter your data. You can create a form from a table or query, or combine data from a number of sources. Forms have a wide variety of controls that display data or add visual interest to the form.

You'll find that forms are especially important when you create an application for inexperienced users. With careful design, you can create forms that guide users through the steps to enter, edit, and get data from your database. Well-designed forms also limit the possibility of data error. See the Frustration Busters box for tips on creating effective forms.

FRUSTRATION BUSTERS!

A perennial danger with any database is that users will enter data incorrectly. By carefully designing the forms that others use to enter, edit, or review data, you can avoid many problems. Some things to consider when designing a form are the following:

■ If users will be entering data from a specific source, such as a paper form, match your form's design to the paper counterpart. Users are more likely to enter data correctly if they don't have to search for each piece of it.

■ Use rectangles and lines to group sets of controls. This way, users enter related data (such as all of a product's identification information or an entire address) together.

■ Don't crowd together the controls, making them hard to read. Users need to be able to easily identify which control they are working with.

■ Make sure that the text on the form is meaningful and concise. Two text box controls labeled "Name" won't help a user enter an employee's first and last name correctly.

■ Use validation rules to help ensure that entries occur in a logical range. For example, if you know that billing rates in your company vary from $50 to $300 an hour, you can assign validation rules to the Hourly Rate control to prevent a $5,000 entry.

■ Use input masks on standardized entries. For example, since you know exactly how many characters are needed to enter a phone number, an input mask, like the one you use in tables, can make that entry easier.

■ Use formatting to make numbers easier to read. It's easier to see that the salary of 1453920.20 is wrong when it looks like $1,453,920.20.

When I click on a command button control that performs a FindRecord action, I get the message "Can't search data using current FindRecord action arguments." What's happening?

The FindRecord action tries to find a record based on the contents of the current control. When you click this button, however, you are transferring the focus to it. Therefore, Access no longer knows what to search for.

To resolve this situation, add a GoToControl action to the macro containing the FindRecord action. This transfers the focus to the control containing the data you want to search for so the FindRecord action can work correctly. Your edited macro may look like this:

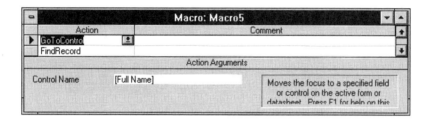

Can I prevent a user from updating records in my form?

Yes, you can easily prevent users from updating the records displayed in your form by setting the AllowUpdating property to No Tables in the form's Design view. This prevents users from editing the contents of controls that are bound to a table or query.

Tech Tip: You can also get similar results by changing the DefaultEditing property to Read Only and the AllowEditing property to Unavailable. The DefaultEditing property sets whether you can edit records when you open a form. Selecting Read Only prevents changes until you choose Allow Editing from the Records menu. Setting the AllowEditing property to Unavailable makes this command unavailable.

Can I prevent users from adding new records in my form?

You can use the DefaultEditing property to prevent users from adding new records. To do this:

1. Open your form in Design view.

2. Display the property sheet for the form by clicking the Properties toolbar button, shown here, or by choosing <u>P</u>roperties from the <u>V</u>iew menu.

3. Move to the Default Editing property and set it to Can't Add Records.

4. Save the form, and then switch back to Form view. You can no longer add records using this form.

Can I open a form without showing a highlight on any field until I've selected a record to edit?

Access offers you two ways to hide the highlight that usually appears in the first control when you open a form.

If you set the Tab Stop property for all of the form's controls to No, no highlight will appear. However, when you do this, you cannot use TAB to move between the controls. Pressing TAB instead moves to the next record, so you have to use the mouse to move between controls. You may not see your edits until you scroll back to the record you just edited. In this form, the control that selects which record appears can have an event procedure that returns the TabStop property for these controls to Yes.

Another option is to add an invisible control that holds the focus. This lets you continue to use TAB to move between controls. To do this:

1. Switch to Design view.

2. Create an unbound text box anywhere in the Detail section of the form by clicking the Text Box Toolbox tool, shown here, and then clicking on the form.

3. Select the control's label and press DEL, assuming that the text box has an attached label.

4. Make the text box control as small as possible so it doesn't interfere with other parts of the form.

5. Open the palette by clicking the Palette toolbar button or by choosing P̲alette from the V̲iew menu.

6. Choose the form's background color for the control's fore color, back color, and border. Now the control blends in with the form's background.

7. Choose Ta̲b Order from the E̲dit menu.

8. Drag the control's name to the top of the Custom Order list box and select OK.

9. Switch to Form view by clicking the Form View toolbar button, shown here, or by choosing F̲orm from the V̲iew menu.

The form displays without any of the visible controls being highlighted, as in Figure 7-1. When you press TAB, you move to the first visible control, which is the second one in the tab order.

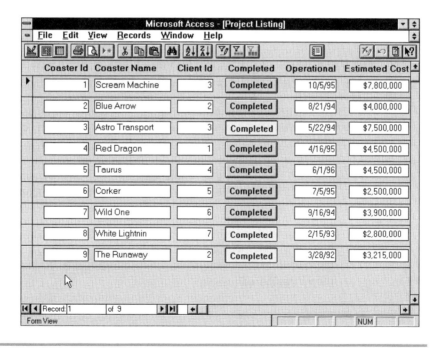

FIGURE 7-1   A form without any visible highlight

Can I create a shortcut for opening my Employees form in Design view?

Yes, you can create an AutoKeys macro group to define shortcut keystrokes. If you want to open the Employees form in Design view each time you press CTRL+E, create a macro in the AutoKeys macro group with the name ^e. This macro's name, ^e, is what the SendKeys action uses to represent CTRL+E. The ^e macro's only action is OpenForm, using the form's name and the view as the arguments, as shown here:

```
Name:    ^e  Action:   OpenForm  Arguments:  Form Name:  Employees
                                                  View:  Design
```

The AutoKeys macro group will execute automatically when you open your database. Once it executes, the shortcut keystroke is available. You can open your Employees form in Design view at any time.

How do I synchronize my forms so that a second form shows the data related to the record in the first form?

To synchronize the data on two related forms, create a macro that opens the second form with a Where Condition as shown next:

```
Action:   OpenForm  Arguments:  Form Name:       Second Form Name
                                 Where Condition:      Condition
```

The condition is usually a control in the second form that you want equal to a value in the first form. For example, if you use the Client ID field to synchronize the two forms, you can enter the following condition:

```
Client ID = Forms![First Form]![Client ID]
```

When the macro opens the second form, this condition sets the control to the appropriate entry, synchronizing the two forms. Figure 7-2 shows two synchronized forms. The "Clients and Their Coasters" form opens the Project Listing form when you click the Display Project Data button. This button has an OnClick property to run the macro that opens the second form.

Another special feature of the two forms shown in Figure 7-2 is that the Project Listing form's OnActivate property runs another macro. The OnActivate property occurs when you switch from another window. This second macro is important because once the Project Listing form is open, you need some way to keep the forms synchronized. When you switch back to the "Clients and Their Coasters" form to show another record, the Project Listing form still shows the same records. Since the second form is already open, you may not want to click the command button to update the Project Listing form. Instead, the second macro performs the ApplyFilter action and refreshes the records shown in the second form. The Where Condition argument for this action is the same one used by the macro that the Display Project Data button performs.

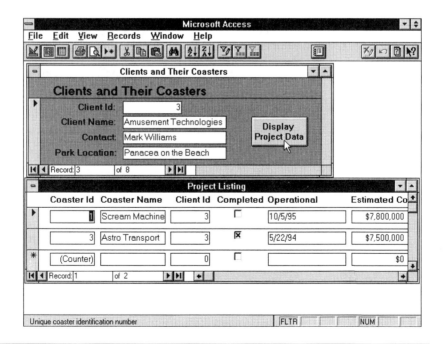

FIGURE 7-2   Two synchronized forms

I used different validation rules for certain fields in my form and table. Which one actually gets used when I enter data in the form?

Actually, both of them apply when you enter data in the form. Access tests the data you enter using both the form's and the table's validation rules. If the data violates either rule, you can't save the record containing the offending data.

Access evaluates a validation rule when you move the focus to another control or record after entering or editing data. If you leave a field without entering or altering any data, the validation rule is not evaluated. Access also tests entries with the validation rules when you leave the form, switch views, or close the form. Since Access doesn't check the validation rules when you leave a control blank, you need to use a macro to find null values.

Can I close a form automatically after a set amount of time?

Yes, you can have a form close itself after a certain amount of time. To do this:

1. Create a macro that executes the Close action on the form.

2. Switch to the form's Design view.

3. Open the property sheet by choosing Properties from the View menu or by clicking the Properties toolbar button.

4. Move to the TimerInterval property, and set it to the number of milliseconds you want the form to stay open. Remember, there are 1,000 milliseconds to 1 second. For example, enter **5000** if you want the form to stay open 5 seconds or **60000** if you want the form opened a minute.

5. Move to the OnTimer event property, and attach the macro with the Close action.

Now, when you open the form, it displays for the time set in the TimerInterval property, and then it closes.

Can I look at the Access Basic code behind a particular form?

While in the form's Design view, choose <u>C</u>ode from the <u>V</u>iew menu or click the Code toolbar button shown here. A Module window appears. To show the code for a specific object, select it from the Object drop-down list box in the toolbar. To see the Access Basic code associated with a specific event for that object, select the event from the Procedure drop-down list box in the toolbar.

Tech Tip: You can also quickly see the code already added to an event property by clicking the Build button at the end of the property in the property sheet.

How do I move the property sheet once I've moved it so high that I can't see its title bar?

You can move the property sheet by using its Control menu. Click one of the properties to select the property sheet. You may even want to select an empty one to make sure you don't accidentally remove the entry. While in the property sheet, press ALT+SPACEBAR, and then press ENTER to choose <u>M</u>ove from the Control menu. Then use the arrow keys to move the property sheet. When it is in a good spot, press ENTER again.

How do I create a shadow box on a form like the one the Form Wizard creates?

The shadow boxes that the Form Wizard creates are actually two rectangle controls. One control is the box, the other is its shadow. You can use the same technique to provide shadows for other controls, such as text boxes and combo boxes. In these cases, you use the control as the first rectangle and simply create the second rectangle as the shadow itself. To create a shadowed box:

1. With the form in Design view, create a rectangle around the controls you want inside the shadow box. If you are adding a shadow to another type of control, create that control.

2. Choose <u>D</u>uplicate from the <u>E</u>dit menu to create a second rectangle control.

3. Move the second rectangle slightly to the right of and below the first one.

4. With the second rectangle still selected, open the Palette by clicking the Palette toolbar button, shown here, or by choosing P<u>a</u>lette from the <u>V</u>iew menu.

5. Click the color for the shadow under Back Color.

6. Choose Send to <u>B</u>ack from the F<u>o</u>rmat menu.

Figure 7-3 shows a form with three shadows created by adding rectangle controls. The rectangles for the shadows have all the same properties as the other rectangle controls except for the Left, Top, and BackColor properties.

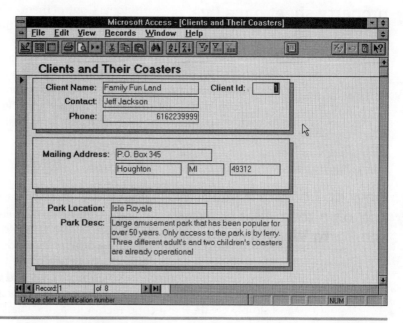

FIGURE 7-3   A form decorated with shadows

Can I let users of a form easily cancel out of entering a record?

To cancel a new record, a user would press ESC twice. To automate this function, create a macro for a command button that they can press to undo the entered record. This macro uses the SendKeys action to send two ESC keystrokes. The macro might look like:

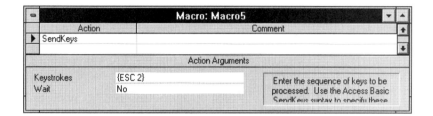

Add this macro to the OnClick property of a command button on the form.

Tech Tip: You can add command buttons with the Control Wizard that will undo the currently entered record. After you place the button on the form's design, select Record Operations from the Categories list box and Undo Record from the When Button Is Pressed list box. From the next dialog box, the Control Wizard suggests one of these three pictures for the button that you create when you select Finish.

Can I create something on my form like the ToolTips labels that appear when I point my mouse at a toolbar button?

Yes. You can hide the labels for your controls and then set them to appear when the user moves to that control. This way the name or instructions for a control only appear when the user is working with that control. To do this:

1. Create the labels you want to appear when each control is active.

Tech Tip: Remember to set the font name, size, and weight for the text as well as the color and border. If these labels look too much like other controls in the form, they won't look like Access' ToolTips. You can choose the back color for the labels by clicking the Build button at the end of the BackColor property. The Color dialog box that appears offers the same palette that you see when you choose Colors from the Control Panel program. The palette here includes the color of Access' ToolTips that is missing from the Palette window.

2. Select all of the labels you want to appear only when the related control is active.

3. Open the property sheet by clicking the Properties toolbar button or by choosing Properties from the View menu.

4. Set the Visible property of the selected labels to No.

5. Select each control that has a related label and enter the following code as an event procedure to the GotFocus property:

```
Me![Label's Control Name].Visible = -1
```

This procedure makes the label visible when the related control gets the focus. You can click the Build button at the end of the property, and then select Code Builder to open the form's Module window.

6. Enter the following code as an event procedure to the OnLostFocus property for the controls that have a related label:

```
Me![Label's Control Name].Visible = 0
```

This procedure hides the label when the related control loses the focus.

Your form's design might look like the one in Figure 7-4. You can see the labels that will appear as you move to different text boxes. You can also see the form's Module window showing the event procedure performed when the First Name control gets

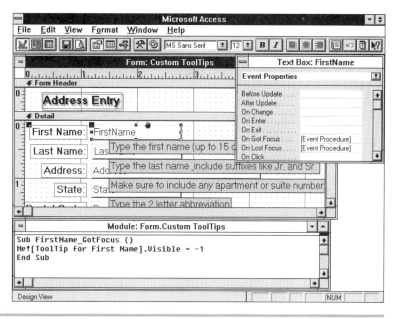

FIGURE 7-4   Form design to show custom ToolTips

the focus. When you display this form and move to the First
Name field, the form looks like this:

When I choose Output **T**o from the **F**ile menu while in a
form, my file is missing the data from the subform.
What's wrong?

This command does not output the data from subforms,
subreports, or graphs. This is simply a part of Access' design and
cannot be worked around.

When I double-click an OLE object in Form view nothing happens. How do I edit this object?

The reason you can't edit the OLE object is that the control's Enabled property is set to No. Access sets the Enabled property differently for OLE objects that are part of the form design versus those stored in a table. The object you double-clicked is probably an unbound OLE object. To edit the unbound OLE object while in Form view, you need to return to the form's Design view. Select the control containing the OLE object and display the property sheet. Move to the Enabled property and set it to Yes. Move to the Locked property and set it to No. From now on, you can edit your unbound OLE objects in Form view. The bound object frames that display OLE objects stored in a table already have their Enabled property set to Yes.

Tech Tip: You can tell in Form view whether you can edit an OLE object. When you can edit the object, it has black marks (handles) around the inside of the frame, as you can see here on the OLE object on the right:

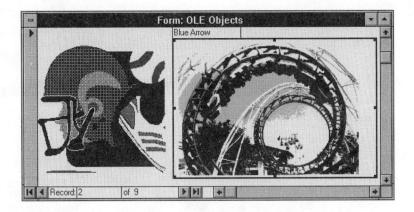

Tech Tip: When the OLE object is a sound, double-clicking it plays the sound. If it's a video clip, double-clicking will play the video clip. It you want to edit the object when you double-click it, you'll need to change the control's Verb property to -1 or -2 while you are in the form's design.

Can I invoke Access Basic code within a form?

Yes, you can execute Access Basic code within a form. To do this for a Function procedure, you need to call the function from a property of the form or a control in it. To do so, move to the property, and enter

```
=FunctionName()
```

You can also perform Access Basic code in a form by attaching event procedures to the form or to the controls on the form. Event procedures are Sub procedures.

Tech Tip: Some properties cannot use Sub procedures. If you want to run a Sub procedure, you need to add a Function procedure that performs the Sub procedure.

If I export a form to another Access database, are the procedures that the form uses also exported?

When you export a form, the form's design includes its module containing all the event procedures. If the form only uses event procedures, your form design has all the ones you need. If the form uses procedures from other modules, these procedures are not included. To get those procedures into the other database, export the module they are contained in.

Can I test to find the view my form is in?

You may need to know a form's current view in a macro or in an Access Basic procedure. The CurrentView property indicates which view the form is using. This property is only available in macros or Access Basic code. The possible settings for this property are

0	Design view
1	Form view
2	Datasheet view

As an example, a macro can have a condition to test the current view. This entry might look like:

```
Forms![Form Name].CurrentView = 1
```

Then when the current view is the Form view, the macro will perform some action.

How do I find all other records in a form that match the current values of two controls on the form?

You need to have Access filter the records that appear in the form. You can create a macro that applies a filter or that opens a form with a specific filter. Select the property of the event that causes the records to be chosen. For a command button, you want the OnClick property. For example, we'll assume that the form has two controls named Entry 1 and Entry 2 in the Enter Address form, containing the entries for which you want to find a match. Also, we'll assume that they match the City and State field controls in the other form. The macro that applies the filter to the current form has the ApplyFilter action and a Where Condition argument of:

```
[City]=[Forms]![Enter Address]![Entry 1] And [State]=
[Forms]![Enter Address]![Entry 2]
```

If the macro needs to open the form as well, change the action to OpenForm, and enter the form name for the Form Name argument.

Can I prevent users from closing my form with the Control-menu box?

Yes, in fact, you can remove the Control-menu box from the Form window. This way, you can make sure that users only exit the form the way you intended. To do so, open the form in Design view. View the form's properties, and then set the ControlBox property to No. Your form might look like Figure 7-5.

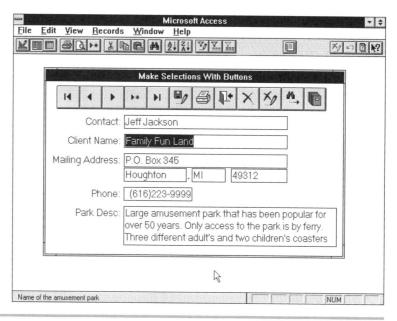

FIGURE 7-5   Form without a Control-menu box, scroll bars, or navigation buttons

Can I hide the scroll bars and navigation buttons in my forms?

Yes, on forms you can hide these elements by changing the ScrollBars and NavigationButtons properties. View the form's properties by selecting Properties from the View menu. Move to the ScrollBars property and enter Neither. Then select the NavigationButtons property and enter No. Your form might look like the one in Figure 7-5.

Besides hiding the scroll bars and navigation buttons, you can hide the record selectors by setting the RecordSelectors property to No. You can remove the Minimize, Maximize, and Restore buttons in the upper-right corner of the form by changing the MinButton and MaxButton properties to No.

Tech Tip: If you want to hide the navigation buttons and scroll bars on a subform, you have to modify the subform's design and change the properties there. You cannot hide the navigation buttons and scroll bars for a form's datasheet.

In my form, I compare a calculated field to a numeric field. Even when the values appear the same, Access says they're not equal. What's going on?

Your calculated value probably has digits after the decimal point that do not display because of the format. You need to eliminate those extra digits. You can create a function that truncates the trailing digits or one that rounds to a set decimal place. The following functions can truncate or round your numbers to two digits after the decimal point.

```
Function RndC(X)
RndC = Int (X * Factor + 0.5) / Factor
End Function

Function TruncC(X)
TruncC = Int (X * Factor) / Factor
End Function
```

To use either function, you need the following line added to the Declarations section of the module:

```
Const Factor = 100
```

The Factor constant, currently set as 100, sets the number of digits after the decimal point. The number of 0's after the 1 is the number of digits that the function's result displays after the decimal point. Either function can be used like Access' built-in functions. For example, a control on a form that displays one of two messages based on whether the values of Commission Due and Commission Paid are the same might look like this:

```
IIf(RndC([Commission Due])=RndC([Commission Paid]), "All
Commissions Paid", "Commission Still Due: " & Format
(RndC([Commission Due]-[Commission Paid]), "Currency")
```

Tech Tip: Another possibility is that the values are different data types. Check whether one of the values you are comparing is stored as a string and the other is stored as a number. If Access stores one as a string, use the Val function to convert it to a number. For example, if First Number contains 68 and Second Number contains "68", the expression that tests whether the two numbers are the same is [First Number]=Val([Second Number]).

Can I move between the header and detail sections of a form without a mouse?

Yes. Just press F6 to move between the sections of a form.

Can I open a second form by selecting its name from a combo box in the first form?

Yes, you can open one form by selecting its name from a combo box in another form. You first need to create a combo box containing the names of all the forms in your database. Then you need to set it up so that selecting a name from this combo box opens the selected form. To do this, you use Access Basic.

1. Create the combo box from which you want to select the form to open on the first form.

2. Display the property sheet for your combo box.

3. Enter **ListofForms** for the combo box's Name property.

4. Select **Value List** as the RowSourceType property setting.

5. Move to the OnEnter property, then click the Builder button at the end of the field.

6. Select Code Builder in the list box, then click OK.

7. Enter the following code:

```
Sub ListofForms_Enter ()
Dim Mydb As Database
Dim MyContainer As Container
Dim I as Integer
Dim List As String
Set Mydb = DBEngine.Workspaces(0).Databases(0)
Set MyContainer = Mydb.Containers("Forms")
list = ""
For I = 0 To MyContainer.Documents.Count - 1
    List = List & MyContainer.Documents(I).Name & ";"
Next I
Me![ListofForms].RowSource = Left(List, Len(List) - 1)
End Sub
```

8. Close the Module window.

9. Move to the combo box's AfterUpdate property, and select the Build button again.

10. Select Code Builder from the list box and click OK.

11. Enter the following code:

```
Sub ListofForms_AfterUpdate ()
    DoCmd OpenForm Me![ListofForms]
End Sub
```

12. Close the Module window.

13. Open the form in Form view and select a value from the combo box. The form you select is opened.

Can I add a button to a form to move me to the end of a table so I can enter new records?

Yes, you can easily create such a command button in your forms. In fact, Access 2.0 will give you a hand with its Command Button Wizard. To add this button to the form's design:

1. Select Command Wizards from the View menu, or click the Control Wizards Toolbox button, shown here, if the Control Wizards are turned off.

2. Select the Command Button tool from the Toolbox.

3. Click the form where you want the command button to appear. Access now starts the Command Button Wizard.

4. Select Record Operations from the Categories list box and Add New Records from the When Button Is Pressed list box.

5. Select Finish.

6. Display the property sheet for this command button control.

7. Move to the OnClick property, and then click the Build button. The form's Module window opens and displays the event procedure created by the Command Button Wizard.

8. Move to the end of the line that reads DoCmd GoToRecord , , A_NEWREC and press ENTER.

9. Type **Forms!*Form Name!*[*Control Name*].SetFocus** where *Form Name* is the name of your form and *Control Name* is the name of the first control in your tab order.

Now when you select the command button in the form, Access moves you to a blank new record, and moves the focus to the first control in your tab order.

Can I convert a form into a report?

Yes, you can easily convert a form into a report. Just open the form in Design view, and then choose Save As Report from the File menu.

Why doesn't the header that I created appear in Form view?

The header you created was probably a page header. There are two headers available on forms: form headers and page headers. A form header appears both on the screen and when printed, but a page header displays only if the form is printed. The same is true for the page footer.

Tech Tip: To display the Page Header and Page Footer sections, choose Page Header/Footer from the Format menu. To display the Form Header and Form Footer sections, choose Form Header/Footer from the Format menu.

How can I use the ActiveForm property while I am opening a form?

The only way to reference a form using the ActiveForm property is to bypass the actual events occurring when a form opens and call it from the OnTimer property. For example, you can display a message when the form opens showing the form's Name property. To do this, assuming that the form's name is Categories, add this code to the OnOpen property:

```
Forms![Categories].TimerInterval = 1
```

In the OnTimer property of the form, add this code:

```
Dim MyForm As Form
Set MyForm = Screen.ActiveForm
MsgBox "Now opening " & MyForm.Name
Forms![Categories].TimerInterval = 0
```

This example returns the Name property of the Categories form in a message box like the one shown here and then resets the TimerInterval property to 0.

Reports

Reports in Access are descriptions of how you want to print the data in a table or query. Unlike forms, they aren't displayed on the screen, and cannot be used to enter data. You can create a report manually, or you can use one of Access' Report Wizards to guide you through the process.

Because reports contain many specific sections, understanding what these sections are and how they relate to each other is essential. The following Frustration Busters box summarizes the various sections in an Access report.

FRUSTRATION BUSTERS!

Creating reports can be very confusing at first. However, once you know where and in what order the sections print, you'll find it much easier to create an effective report. A report can contain the following sections:

- *Report Header*—Appears at the beginning of the report.

- *Page Header*—Appears at the top of every page and below any Report Header.

- *Group Header*—Appears before the detail section of the first record of every group.

- *Detail*—Repeats for each record in the report.

- *Group Footer*—Appears after the detail section of the last record of every group.

- *Page Footer*—Appears at the bottom of every page.

- *Report Footer*—Appears at the end of the report.

When Access assembles your report for display or printing, it starts by printing the report header and page header sections. Then it prints the detail section until the page is full. Next Access prints the page footer section, a page break, and the page header section on the next page. Each page contains the page header section, as many detail sections as can fit, and the page footer section. On the last page of the report, the report footer prints before the page footer section. In Figure 8-1, you can see a report design that prints the report previewed in Figure 8-2. You can see how the sections in the report design are added to the final report.

When a report has group sections, the printing order is basically the same. The difference is that Access prints the group header section before the first record of each group, and the group footer section after the last record of each group.

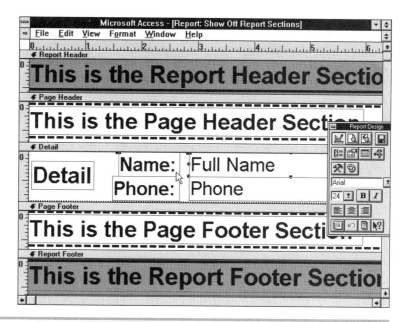

FIGURE 8-1   Report design showing the different sections of a report

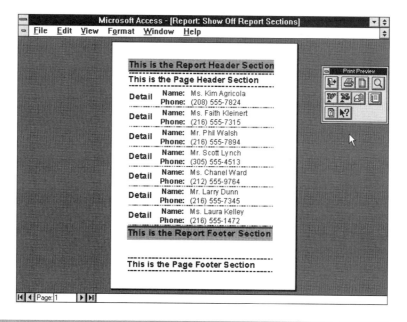

FIGURE 8-2   Report showing how the different sections actually print

Do I have to sort by a field I use to group data in a report?

In Access 2.0, you can use a field or an expression to group your records. The field or expression that groups records sorts them as well. If Access didn't sort the records by the same expression used for grouping, your report would have several groups for the same field or expression value. For example, when you group your customer records by state, you don't want the customers to appear like this:

First Name	Last Name	City	State
Employees In: NY			
Chanel	Ward	Malverne	NY
Employees In: OH			
Faith	Kleinert	Kent	OH
Employees In: CT			
Kim	Agricola	Brookfield	CT
Employees In: OH			
Larry	Dunn	Lorain	OH

Instead, you want your records sorted by the same field or expression used for grouping, so that the preceding records look like this:

First Name	Last Name	City	State
Employees In: CT			
Kim	Agricola	Brookfield	CT
Employees In: FL			
Scott	Lynch	Wilton Manors	FL
Employees In: NY			
Chanel	Ward	Malverne	NY
Employees In: OH			
Larry	Dunn	Lorain	OH
Laura	Kelley	Mentor	OH
Faith	Kleinert	Kent	OH
Phil	Walsh	Eastlake	OH

I used a parameter query as a basis for my report. How can I display the parameter values I enter in the report?

When you create the parameter query, include the parameters themselves as fields in the QBE grid. For example, if you are entering a start date and an end date as the parameters for the

Date field, you should create Start and End fields in the QBE grid, as shown here:

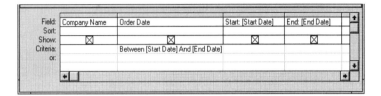

Now when you create your report, the field list for this query displays the two new fields. These fields contain the entries you made for the parameters. You can add them to your report just as you would add any other field from the query.

For example, a text box control can join text and the parameter entries to tell readers what dates are covered by the data in the report. In this case, the expression entered for the control's ControlSource property is

```
= "For the Fiscal Quarter Beginning " & [Start] &
" and Ending " & [End]
```

I want to show a total at the bottom of each page in my report, but I keep seeing #Error instead. What's wrong?

Your problem is that Access does not allow the Sum() function in a page footer. To place a total in a page footer, create a control in another section of your report that performs the calculation. Set its Visible property to No to hide it. You may also need to set its RunningSum property from No to Over All or Over Group to choose when you want the calculation reset. Then create another unbound text box in the page footer. Enter the name of the control containing the calculation as the text box's ControlSource property setting.

As an example, suppose you want to total the billings in the page footer section. Part of your report design might look like the following one. This detail section includes a calculated control that totals the billings. It has its Visible property set to

No and its RunningSum property set to Over All. This control is named Total Calc. The control containing =[Total Calc] in the page footer section returns the value of the Total Calc control for the last record printed on the page, which also is the total up to that point in the report. This control will not show only the running sum for the page.

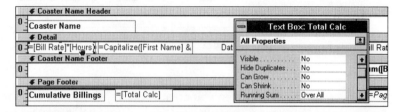

Tech Tip: You can get similar results by adding a macro to the page footer section's OnFormat property. The Item argument equals the control in the page footer section, and the Expression argument equals the control in the other section.

Can I number the records in the detail section of my report?

You can number records within each group or across the entire report. To do so:

1. Add an unbound text box control to the Detail section of the report.

2. Display the properties for this control by clicking the Properties toolbar button, shown here, or by choosing Properties from the View menu.

3. Move to the ControlSource property and enter =**1**.

4. Move to the Running Sum property and set it to Over All.

If you have grouped the records in your report and want to start numbering records again at the beginning of each group, set this property to Over Group instead. The records in your report are numbered, as in Figure 8-3.

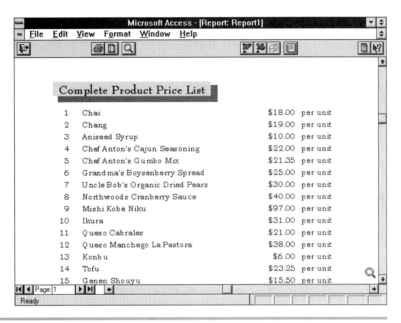

FIGURE 8-3   Numbering records in a report

Is there an easy way to create a tabular report in Access 2.0?

Yes, you can easily create a tabular report by using the Tabular Report Wizard. Click the New Report toolbar button, shown here, while in the Database window, or select the Report tab and click New. Choose the table or query you want to base your report on, and then select Report Wizards. Choose the Tabular Report Wizard and select OK to start creating the report.

Access's AutoReport can create a tabular report if you change one of the options for this Report Wizard. To do this:

1. Choose Add-ins from the File menu while in the Database window and select Add-in Manager.

2. Select Forms and Reports Wizards from the Available Libraries and choose Customize.

3. Select Customize AutoReport, and then select OK to open the AutoReport Style dialog box.

4. Choose Tabular under Layout to switch AutoReport from creating single-column reports to tabular ones.

5. Select OK and Close.

Once you make this change, just highlight that table or query in the Database window and click the AutoReport toolbar button, shown here. This automatically creates a tabular report that includes all of the fields in the selected table or query.

How do I get my report to print multiple columns?

First decide how many columns you want and how much room you have on the page. Once you are sure that all of the columns will fit on the page:

1. Open the report in Design view.

2. Choose Print Setup from the File menu, and then select More.

3. Enter the number of columns you want to create in the Items Across text box.

4. Enter the space you want between the columns in the Column Spacing text box.

Choose whether you want the items arranged vertically or horizontally. When you arrange them horizontally (left to right), you are creating a layout like mailing labels. If you use a vertical layout (top to bottom), they are arranged in columns like text in a newspaper.

5. Select OK twice.

Tech Tip: If you add more than one column to a report and the new column either does not appear or only partially appears, you need to fix the report design. The report width is too wide.

I want my report to use two columns for the Detail section and one column for the other sections. How do I do this?

To create a report that uses different numbers of columns for different sections, you need to use subreports. Figure 8-4 shows a report with a banner at the top and bottom, and a two-column middle section. To create a report like this:

1. Create a report that shows only the details that you want to appear in the final report. Make sure you leave the Report Header, Page Header, Page Footer, and Report Footer sections empty.

Tech Terror: Make sure your report is no wider than the columns you plan to create. If you create columns that are narrower than your report, Access doesn't compress your report; it just doesn't print the controls outside the column's width.

2. Choose Print Setup from the File menu, and then select More.

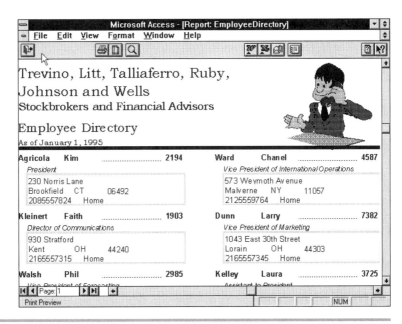

FIGURE 8-4   Using a subreport control to vary the number of columns in one report

3. Enter the number of columns you want to create in the Items Across text box.

4. Enter the space you want between the columns in the Column Spacing text box.

   Choose whether you want the items arranged vertically or horizontally. When you arrange them horizontally (left to right), you are creating a layout like mailing labels. If you use a vertical layout (top to bottom), they are arranged in columns like text in a newspaper.

5. Select OK twice.

6. Save this first report. Assuming you used a vertical orientation with two columns, your first report might look like Figure 8-5.

7. Create another report.

8. Create the headings and footers that span the columns in the first report.

9. Switch to the Database window. Don't maximize it.

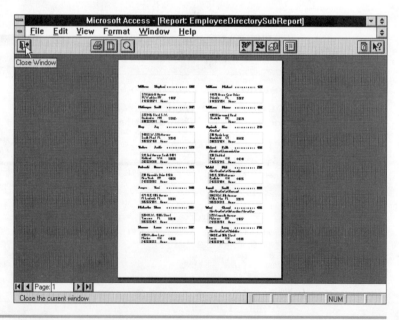

FIGURE 8-5   Creating a multicolumn subreport

10. Drag the first report to the Detail section of the second one.

11. Resize the subreport control, if necessary, so it is as wide as the second report. Figure 8-6 shows the completed main report design. You can see how this report contains the page header section that you want to span the columns. When you switch from here to the preview, your final report might look like Figure 8-4.

Tech Tip: If you have a problem with the main report, make sure that the RecordSource property for the main control is empty. You do not want a table or query associated with this report. For the subreport control, make sure that the LinkChildField and LinkMasterField properties are empty.

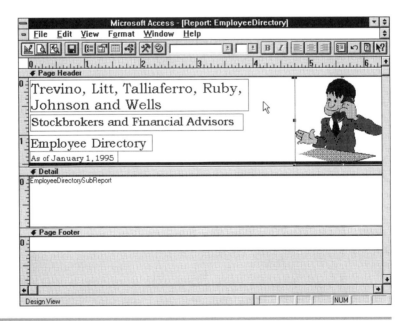

FIGURE 8-6   Creating a one-column main report

Can I start numbering report pages with a number other than one?

Yes, you can start numbering pages at any number that you choose. To do so, add an unbound text box control to the page footer section while in Design view. Display the property sheet for this control, and move to the ControlSource property. Enter

```
=Page+first page number-1
```

How do I change the default print margins?

To change the default print margins, choose Options from the View menu. Select Printing from the Category list box. Enter the new margins in the text boxes below Items and select OK. Access now uses these default print margins for all new reports as well as for printing datasheets, modules, and forms.

If you want to change the print margins for an existing report, you have to do so manually. Open each report in turn. Choose Print Setup from the File menu. Then set the print margins and select OK.

How many headers and footers can I have in a report?

In Access 2.0, you can have one report header and footer, one page header and footer, and up to ten group headers and footers.

How long can my report be?

A report section cannot be any longer than 22 inches. You can include as many sections as you want. Therefore, your complete report can be as long as you need it to be.

Why are some of my report's calculated fields empty?

A calculated field that displays an empty result includes a field entry that equals Null. Calculated fields that use the arithmetic operators (+, -, *, /, \, ^ or Mod) return Null when part of the expression equals Null. To correct this, convert the nulls to zeros by using the NullToZero function included in the sample Northwind database. The NullToZero function looks like this:

```
Function NullToZero (anyValue As Variant) As Variant
' Accepts: a variant value
' Purpose: converts null values to zeros
' Returns: a zero or non-null value
' From: User's Guide Chapter 17

    If IsNull(anyValue) Then
        NullToZero = 0
    Else
        NullToZero = anyValue
    End If

End Function
```

This function converts any null values into zeros so they will not affect the calculation. To use this function, enter the NullToZero function in your database. Then display the property sheet for the calculated control. Edit the ControlSource property so the NullToZero function converts the entry that contains Null values. For example, if a control displays the results of = [Commission Due] - [Commission Paid], change the ControlSource property to

```
= NullToZero([Commission Due]) - NullToZero([Commission Paid])
```

Tech Tip: You can bring this function procedure into your database by importing the Utility module from the Northwind database.

How can I print a report based on the current record in my form?

You need to create a macro that opens a report by using the contents of a control on your form to choose which records display. Attach this macro to the form's command button control so you can open the report by clicking the button.

This macro uses the OpenReport action. Set a Where Condition argument to make the report display the same record currently displayed in the form. For example, this macro might contain the following information:

```
Action:  OpenReport
Arguments:  Report Name:      Name Of Report
            View:             Print
            Where Condition:  [Field Name] = Forms!
                              [FormName]![FormControlName]
```

Field Name is the name of the table or query field that selects which records appear in the report. It must equal the same entry as one of the controls in the form. Attach this macro to the OnClick property of the command button. When you click the command button on your form, Access prints a report using all records with the same value as on the form. If you want the report to show only the record in the form, make sure that the field name contains an entry that is unique to the record. You could use a Counter field, which is unique for each record.

Can I force a page break in the Detail section of a report?

Assuming that the report is not sorting and grouping its records, you can force a page break as follows:

1. Open the report in Design view.
2. Select the Page Break tool in the toolbox.
3. Place the page break in the Detail section where you want it.

4. Create a new macro group. The macro has this information:

```
Macro Name: Hide Page Break
Action:  SetValue  Argument:  Item:   [Form Name]![Page Break
                                       Control Name].Visible
                             Expression:  No
Macro Name: Show Page Break
Action:  SetValue  Argument:  Item:   [Form Name]![Page Break
                                       Control Name].Visible
                             Expression:  Yes
```

5. Save the macro group and switch back to the report design.

6. Specify the first macro in the OnFormat property of the Page Header section. Remember to type the macro group name, a period, and then **Hide Page Break**.

7. Specify the second macro in the OnFormat property of the Detail section. Remember to type the macro group name, a period, and then **Show Page Break**.

Now when you print the report, the page break control alternates when it is visible as the Hide Page Break and Show Page Break macros perform.

Can I choose not to print a section of my report, depending on a specific condition?

Yes, you can attach a macro to the OnFormat property of the section that executes the CancelEvent action when a condition is met. Since the CancelEvent action prevents Access from formatting the section, it doesn't print with the rest of the report.

For example, suppose you don't want to print the Month of Order footer when there is less than $1,000 in sales that month. To do this, create a macro that has a CancelEvent action and the following entry in the Condition column:

```
DSum("[Sale Amount]","[Invoices]","[Month of Order Date] =
Reports![My Report]![Month Text Box]")<1000
```

This condition sums the Sale Amount field in the Invoices table when the Month of Order Date field entry is the same as the contents of the Month Text Box control in the header of the report. When this sum is less than 1000, Access executes the CancelEvent action, so that this section is neither formatted nor printed.

Can I use data in my tables to create mailing labels?

Creating mailing labels from the data in your database is very easy. Access 2.0 includes a Mailing Label Report Wizard that walks you through the process.

1. Open a new report by clicking the New Report toolbar button, or by selecting the Report tab in the Database window, and then selecting New.

2. Choose the table or query containing the data you want to use from the Select A Table/Query drop-down list box.

3. Select Report Wizards.

4. Select Mailing Label in the list box and OK.

5. Create the contents of your mailing label in the Label Appearance box by using fields, punctuation, and text. Select Next.

Figure 8-7 shows a completed Label Appearance box. In the right side of the dialog box, you can see where the fields, punctuation, or text will appear on the label.

6. Select one or more fields to use in sorting the labels. Select Next.

7. Select the size of the labels you are printing and then Next.

8. Select the font used to print the labels and then Next.

9. Select Finish to create and preview your mailing labels. Figure 8-8 shows the preview of the labels designed in Figure 8-7.

Tech Tip:
Depending on the size of your labels and font, you may get a message that the labels don't have enough space. That is why it is important that you preview the labels you create.

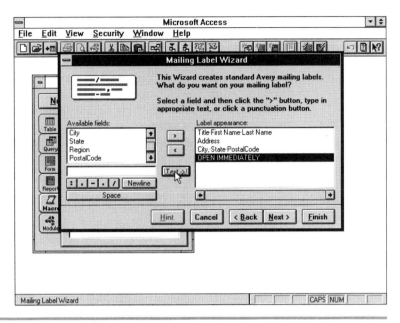

FIGURE 8-7   Creating a mailing label report with the Mailing Label Wizard

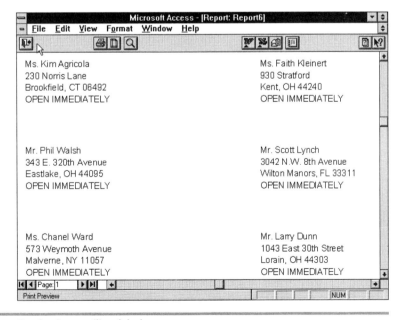

FIGURE 8-8   Previewing mailing labels

Why do I get a block of blank mailing labels?

You may have blank records in the underlying table on which the report is based. If all of the blank records are printing together, then they all contain the same entry in whichever field you are using for sorting. You'll need to check if these blank records are the result of a data entry error, or if these records just won't have entries in those fields. If the records share a trait that causes them not to have entries in these fields, you can define a query that excludes them.

The Mailing Label Wizard created continuous mailing labels. When I preview the report, only one page appears. How can I fix it?

You can view all of the labels by changing the CanShrink property setting of the report's Detail section to Yes. This problem occurs because this section's CanShrink property is set to No. The report may also have some unnecessary space.

I can see mailing labels for all of my records in Print Preview. However, when I use a dot-matrix printer, only the first page of labels prints. What can I do?

There are two possible solutions to your problem. If the first solution doesn't work, try the second.

- In the report's Design view, choose Print Setup from the File menu. Select More. Enter **0.00** in the Row Spacing text box. Select OK and then Close.

- In the report's Design view, open the property sheet for the Detail section. Move to the NewRowOrCol property and set it to After Section.

How do I change the field that sorts my mailing labels?

The same sorting and grouping features that change the order of records in a report also set the order of mailing labels when that is what the report prints. With the report in Design view, open the Sorting and Grouping box by clicking the Sorting and Grouping toolbar button, shown here, or by choosing Sorting and Grouping from the <u>V</u>iew menu. Enter the name of the field by which you want to sort in the Field/Expression column of the first line. Select the kind of sort you want, ascending or descending, in the Sort Order column of the same line. Include any other fields you want to sort by in the following lines.

What can I do if the Mailing Label Report Wizard doesn't list my mailing label size?

You can simply create your own. To do this:

1. Choose Add-<u>I</u>ns from the <u>F</u>ile menu and then select <u>A</u>dd-in Manager.

2. Select Form and Report Wizards from the Available <u>L</u>ibraries list box and then choose <u>C</u>ustomize.

3. Select Customize Mailing Label Sizes from the <u>C</u>ustomize list box and then OK.

4. Select <u>N</u>ew.

5. Enter a label name and the various measurements for your labels in the New Mailing Label dialog box as shown in Figure 8-9.

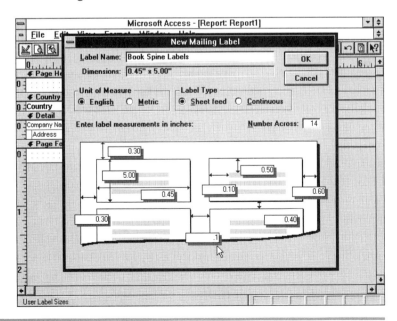

FIGURE 8-9   Dialog box to enter a new label size

6. When you finish, choose OK and then select Close twice.

From now on, the mailing label you just entered is available when you use the Mailing Label Wizard.

Can I create a report that prints a specific number of duplicate mailing labels?

Yes, you can create a report that lets you choose how many copies of each label you want to print. To do so, create a parameter query that makes as many copies of each record as you need:

1. Create a table that contains a single Number type field, with a field size of Integer. For this example, assume that you named the field Number and the table Copies.

2. Create a series of records in the Copies table. The first record should contain one, and each record after it should equal the preceding entry plus one. For example, enter 1, 2, 3, 4, and so forth.

3. Create a query containing all of the information you want to print on your mailing labels. Include the Number field from the Copies table.

  If you switch to Datasheet view, you can see that Access has created a copy of each record for each entry in the Copies table. Since the two tables are unrelated, Access creates a *Cartesian product*, by matching every record in the Copies table to every record in the other table. To print all copies of one label before printing any of the next, sort on a field in the address, such as a Last Name field. Otherwise, you will print one of each label, and then start again.

4. Enter a parameter criterion for the Number field that equals the number of labels you want to print, such as <=[How many copies?]. "How many copies?" is the message Access displays each time this query is run, requesting the entry for this criterion.

5. Create your mailing label report by using the query you just created.

Whenever you attempt to print your report, Access first runs the query. Since it is a parameter query, you get the prompt that lets you choose how many labels to create.

Tech Note: If you use this method to print multiple labels, you'll need to enter as many records in the Copies table as copies you expect to need. If you only add ten records, but want to print 20 copies of labels, you'll have a problem.

 How do I make my report tell users that there are no records to print when the report's query returns no records?

You need to create a macro that counts the number of records in the query's dynaset. The macro displays a message box when the query has no records, or prints the report when the query has some records. You can then attach this macro to the OnOpen property of the report, so it runs when you open the report. Your macro will look like this one:

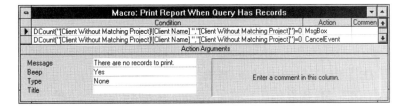

In this macro, DCount first checks whether the field named Client Name in the Client Without Matching Project query contains any entries. Make sure you use a field that must have an entry in each record, such as your primary key. When the query has no records, the MsgBox action displays a message. Then the CancelEvent action cancels the OnOpen event, which prevents opening an empty report. When the query has records, the conditions are false, the macro actions are not performed, and Access continues displaying the report.

How can I print my report to a text file?

Printing your report to a text file in Access is very easy. Simply select your report name from the Database window. Then select Outpu_t_ To from either the _F_ile menu or the shortcut menu. Choose MS-DOS text (*.txt) from the Choose _F_ormat list box and select OK. Type a filename for the output file and select OK again. You have now created a text file of your report.

Tech Tip: If your report includes some unknown characters, change the printer driver to Generic/Text Printer.

How do I summarize calculated fields on a Report?

To summarize a calculated control such as for a report footer section, enter the calculation in the Sum() function. For example, suppose you have a control named Total Billing that has a ControlSource property of =[Billing Rate]*[Hours]. The control in the report footer section that totals this field has a ControlSource property of =Sum([Billing Rate]*[Hours]).

Can I sort the data in a report by a field not displayed on my report?

You can sort by a field not displayed in your report, as long as the field is included in the table or query that you based the report on. To sort by an undisplayed field, simply open the Sorting and Grouping window and include the field in that window. You can open this window either by clicking the Sorting and Grouping button, or by choosing _S_orting and Grouping from the _V_iew menu.

If the field you want to sort by is not included in the table or query you are using, you need to add it. If you are using a query, you can just edit the query to include this field. If you based the report on a table, you need to create a query that displays all of the fields you want to use in the report. Then open the property sheet for the report and enter this new query's name as the RecordSource property setting.

Can I keep groups together on a page, rather than letting them get split between pages?

You can keep groups of records together on a single page. To do this, open the Sorting and Grouping window by clicking the Sorting and Grouping toolbar button, or by choosing Sorting and Grouping from the View menu. Move to each of the fields creating the groups you want to keep together, and then move to the KeepTogether property in the bottom half of the window and set it to Yes.

The KeepTogether property here is the same as the KeepTogether property on the property sheet, except you have one more option. You can choose With First Detail for the KeepTogether property from the Sorting and Grouping window when you want the group's header section on the same page as the first record in the group. This option prevents the unpleasant result of a group header at the bottom of one page and the group's records on the next.

Tech Tip: You can keep entire records on a single page by selecting the Detail section of your report, opening the property sheet, and setting the KeepTogether property to Yes.

Controls Used in Forms and Reports

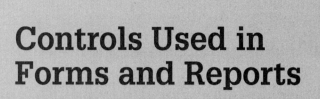

Controls are what you use to define how a report or form will look. They shape the appearance of the data and add other visual elements. The controls you use in forms and reports are basically the same. All the questions in this chapter are about problems with either type of design.

FRUSTRATION BUSTERS!

Access offers many types of controls. Some work better in forms than reports. Other control types are chosen because they work better in displaying specific data. Here are the types of controls you can add to forms and reports, along with some ideas about when to use them.

- *Label*—Adds text that doesn't change from record to record. You can use labels to add fixed information such as a company or department name, or to label data.

- *Text Box*—Accepts or displays text that changes from record to record. This type of control is commonly used to display and enter data. The control displays the contents of a single field, just as you would see it in the table's datasheet.

- *Option Group*—Contains a group of toggle buttons, option buttons, or check boxes. Option groups hold other types of controls, such as toggle buttons or option buttons.

- *Toggle Button*—Shows a button that can look pressed or released just like the Design View and Datasheet View toolbar buttons. Toggle buttons are usually used with Yes/No type fields. Toggle buttons, option buttons, or check boxes can be used interchangeably. Use these controls to show a field's contents when there are limited possible entries.

- *Option Button*—Shows a round option button that can be selected. Option buttons usually show the selected entry when a limited set exists. They can also be used with Yes/No type fields.

- *Check Box*—Shows a square box that contains an X when selected. Check boxes frequently display the setting of a Yes/No type field. However, you can also use them in place of option buttons or toggle buttons to show the entry for a field.

- *Combo Box*—Shows a drop-down list box like the ones in dialog boxes. Forms frequently use them to give you a choice of typing an entry or selecting one from a list. They also save space because they use less space than a list box. Reports seldom use this type of control.

- *List Box*—Shows a list box with the current selection highlighted. List boxes work well in forms when a user can only select from a predifined set of choices.

- *Graph*—Shows a graph based on data from a table or query. The graph is created using the Microsoft Graph application that comes with Access. The Graph Wizard guides you through creating the graph.

- *Subform/Subreport*—Adds a control representing another form or report. This subform or subreport appears in the form or report you are designing. Use subforms and subreports to show records from a related table that are associated to the record currently displayed in the main form or report.

- *Object Frame*—Adds a control that contains an OLE object. Use this control when you paste data from another application into your form or report design.

- *Bound Object Frame*—Adds a placeholder that displays the contents of OLE Object fields. Use this control to see embedded and linked pictures.

- *Line*—Adds a line. Use lines to divide or decorate the form or report.

- *Rectangle*—Adds a box. Add boxes to your design to visually group controls.

- *Page Break*—Adds a page break. Divide a form into multiple pages when you have lots of data to show or enter. Breaking it into smaller chunks makes it easier to understand. Divide reports into pages when you have more data than can fit on one page and you want to control where the page break occurs. Reports have several page break options, so you can place page breaks by section properties instead of with a control.

- *Command Button*—Adds a button that does something when selected, such as executing a macro or module. Unlike toggle buttons, command buttons don't stay pressed.

My Date field has a Long Date format in its table and a Short Date format in a query. When I add the field from the query to my form, what format does it use?

Any field properties you set in the query override the field properties set in the table. Therefore, if you add the field with the Short Date format from the query rather than the field with the Long Date format from the table, the control displaying the date field in the form initially has the Short Date format. In addition, you can use another format in the form without changing the field's Format property for the field in the table or query.

Why doesn't the To Fit command from the submenu displayed when I select Size from the Format menu adjust the size of my controls to fit the text in them?

Choosing Size from the Format menu and then choosing To Fit does adjust the height and width of labels and command and toggle buttons. However, it adjusts only the *height* of text boxes, combo boxes, and list boxes to fit the font of the text it contains. This command does not change the *width* of these controls because the width depends on the control's contents. If you want to change the width of these objects, you must do so manually.

How can I enter a calculated value from a form into my table?

Normally, you don't want to store calculations in a table. Since queries, forms, and reports can display calculated fields so easily, including a calculated field in a table usually indicates a poor database design. However, sometimes it makes sense, such as when you are planning to export that table. Storing calculated values can be done with these few steps:

1. Add the control that calculates the value you want to insert into the table. Enter the calculation as the setting for this control's ControlSource property.

2. Add a bound control for the table field in which you want to enter this calculated value. If you don't want to see this control, change its Visible property to No. This second control must be in the form's design, even if you can't see it.

3. Create a macro with a SetValue action. The Item argument is the name of the control bound to the table's field. The Expression argument is the name of the unbound control that performs the calculation. For example, a macro that will enter the value computed by the ExtPrice control in the Extended Price bound control contains this information:

```
Action: SetValue Arguments: Item: Forms!Form1![Extended Price]
                            Expression: Forms!Form1![ExtPrice]
```

4. Add the macro to the OnCurrent or BeforeUpdate property of the form.

5. Use the form. The macro sets the value of the bound control to the value of the calculated control. This bound control's value is what Access stores in the table field.

Remember that the value entered in the field is the value at the time you use the form. The field does not contain a formula. If the values used in the calculation change, the field will not update itself.

Tech Tip: You can make entering the control names for the macro arguments easier by clicking the Build button at the end of the Item or Expression text box. From the Expression Builder, you can select Forms, Loaded Forms, and the form name to list the controls in the form. Figure 9-1 shows the Expression Builder after selecting the control name. Using the Expression Builder means you don't have to remember the correct order of information and punctuation.

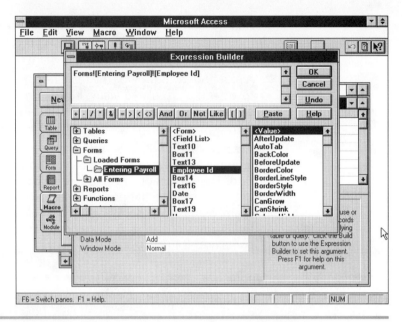

FIGURE 9-1   Selecting a control in a form with the Expression Builder

Can I keep lines straight on reports and forms?

Yes, you can keep your lines straight. Press SHIFT while you drag the mouse to create the line. When SHIFT is pressed, Access creates a straight line that is either horizontal, vertical, or at a 45° angle.

How can I have a text box that combines text along with one or more fields?

A calculated control can combine the text and field contents by *concatenating*, or combining, text. Enter the formula that joins the text and field contents as the ControlSource property for the text box. For example, if you want to combine the First Name and Last Name fields along with some text, the text box might have the following ControlSource property:

```
= "The Employee of the Month is " & [First Name] & " " &
[Last Name]
```

The output of this field will show something like the following, depending on the contents of the First Name and Last Name fields.

```
The Employee of the Month is Scott Lynch
```

How can I move just my label for a text box? They keep moving together.

To move just the label, watch how you select it. Eight small boxes called *handles* surround the label when you select it. The one in the upper-left corner is larger than the others. When you point to the larger handle, the pointer turns into a hand pointing with its index finger, like the one shown here. Drag this larger handle to move just the label. The text box stays where it is.

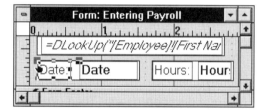

Tech Tip: You can create a compound control, such as the ones created automatically, by adding a label to another control. To add the label, add a separate label control containing the text you want next to the other control. Select the label control, press CTRL+DEL to cut it to the Clipboard, select the control you want the label attached to, and press SHIFT+INS. Both controls in a compound control move together, unless you point to one of the controls as previously described.

I created a form with shadowed text. When I edit the text, however, its shadow doesn't change. How do I edit the shadow text?

Many of the Form and Report Wizards create shadowed text. This text is actually a combination of two label controls. The second label is darker and lower than the first. If you change the top label, the "shadow" doesn't change. To enter the same text in both label controls easily, click the vertical ruler next to the shadowed text. This selects both label controls. Now display the property sheet, and enter the text you want for the Caption property. The text changes for both controls.

How can I prevent users from moving to a control on a form?

Forms have *tab orders* that set the sequence in which you move through the controls on the form by pressing TAB. However, you can take a control out of the tab sequence, so that pressing TAB never moves you to that control. Simply set the control's TabStop property to No. However, regardless of the TabStop property, you can still click the control to move to it.

How can I prevent Access from running a Control Wizard every time I create a button, combo box, or list box?

You can turn off the Control Wizards. When you create a command button, option group, combo box, or list box with the Control Wizards off, you simply add an empty control to the form or report design. You must enter the settings in the property sheet that the Wizard usually fills in based on your responses. To turn off these Wizards, display the Toolbox in the form or report design. Then click the Control Wizards button in the Toolbox, shown here, so it no longer looks depressed. You can also choose Control Wizards in the View menu to turn the Wizards on and off.

How do you open a combo box on a form without a mouse?

Move to the combo box and press ALT+DOWN ARROW.

How can I avoid having to click the down arrow to display the choices in my combo box?

Add a macro to the OnEnter property of the combo box that has a SendKeys action. The macro has this information:

```
Action:   SendKeys   Arguments:   Keystrokes:   %{DOWN}
                                   Wait:   No
```

After you add this macro to the OnEnter property, moving to the combo box triggers this event and runs this macro. This macro sends the keystroke ALT+DOWN ARROW that opens the combo box.

What's the difference between the ControlSource and RowSource properties for a combo box?

These properties describe where the combo box gets the data to display in the drop-down list, and where the entered or selected data goes.

The RowSource property specifies where the combo box gets the information to display in its drop-down list. For example, in a form for entering time card information, the Employee combo box might get its information from the Employee field of the Payroll table.

The ControlSource property specifies where the data selected or entered in the combo box is stored. For example, if the combo box specifies the employee whose time card is being entered, the selection in the combo box is stored in the Employee ID field of the Time Clock table. The field entered for the ControlSource property also sets the entry that appears in the combo box when you look at an existing record.

Do I need to set the ControlSource property for a combo box?

You only need to set the ControlSource property for a combo box when you enter data by using the combo box. When you use it for data entry, the ControlSource property tells Access where to store the data you enter. However, if you use the combo box to find records instead, as in the next two questions, then you don't want to set the ControlSource property—there is no new data to store.

Can I use a combo box on my form to select a record and have the form's information change accordingly?

You can create a macro attached to a combo box's AfterUpdate event that changes the record displayed in a form to the one currently selected in the combo box. The first step is creating the combo box that displays the entries you use to select the record. Next create the macro to assign to the control's AfterUpdate property. The macro will:

- Go to the control on the form that displays the same field as the combo box's entry.

- Find the record equal to the selection from the combo box by applying a filter.

As an example, assume that you want to display a company's record by selecting a company name from the Company Pick List combo box control. The macro for this control's AfterUpdate property contains the following information:

```
Action:       GoToControl
Arguments:    Control Name:   [Company Name]
Action:       FindRecord
Arguments:    Find What:      = [Company Pick List]
```

After you save the macro and switch to Form view, you can choose a company name from the Company Pick List combo box. The macro switches the displayed record to the one selected in the combo box.

Can I use a combo box as a record selector without using a macro?

Yes, you can use a main form/subform link to synchronize a combo box and a form. To do this:

1. Create an unbound form (one that does not have a table or query for its RecordSource property).

2. Add a combo box to the form that lists the entries in a field. These entries are the ones you will use to select which record displays. You can use the Control Wizard to select the data to appear in this control.

3. Create a second form based on the table or query containing your data. This is the form you use to work with the selected record.

4. Save the bound form.

5. Switch back to the first form.

6. Switch to the Database window. You do not want this window maximized.

7. Drag the icon for the second form from the Database window to the first form. Doing this adds the second form to the first one as a subform control.

8. Select the subform control, display the property sheet, and view the Data properties.

9. Set the LinkMasterField property to the control name of the combo box.

10. Set the LinkChildField property to the control name on the form that contains the same information displayed in the combo box.

As an example, Figure 9-2 shows two copies of the same main form so you can see the form both in Design and Form view. In Form view, the combo box lists the contents of the Full Name field. This combo box is an unbound control. When you select a name from this control, the record shown in the bottom of the form changes. The bottom of the form is actually a subform

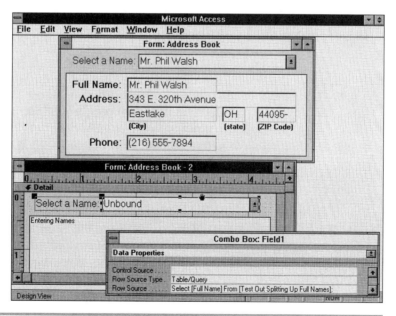

FIGURE 9-2   Linking which report appears according to a combo box's value

control. This subform has a LinkMasterField property of Field1, which is the name of the combo box control. The subform's LinkChildField property is Full Name. This link between the forms is how the subform displays the correct record.

How can you move controls as a group?

To move controls as a group, you need to select all of them. There are two ways to select more than one control in your form or report design.

- Select adjacent controls by dragging the mouse across all of them. Drag the mouse from a point above and to the left of the controls to a position below and to the right of them. You select all controls even partially inside the temporary box you are drawing.

- Hold down SHIFT and click each control to move.

The selected controls can then be moved, sized, or aligned as a group.

Access underlines the next letter when I enter an "&" in a label. How do I display an "&"?

The ampersand (&) is a special character in Access. It identifies the letter you want underlined. Underlining a letter lets you move to the attached part of a compound control by pressing ALT and a letter. This is just like pressing ALT and a letter to select something in a dialog box. To tell Access that you want the & symbol instead of an underlined letter, simply type two ampersands next to each other. For example, type **Chris && Sandie's Pet Store** to display "Chris & Sandie's Pet Store."

How do I format numbers in my form or report as currency?

You can use two methods to display numbers in forms and reports with dollar signs and with commas to separate thousands. Both methods start by showing the property sheet for the text box control that displays the number.

- Select Currency for the text box's Format property. This method works for both calculated fields and Number type fields.

Tech Tip: When you change the Format property, you may also want to change the DecimalPlaces property. This property sets how many digits appear after the decimal point.

- Use the CCur() data type conversion function to convert a calculated field into a currency value. As an example, suppose the calculation was = [Quantity] * [Amount]. This calculation returns an unformatted number such as 7.59. If you change the ControlSource property to = CCur([Quantity] * [Amount]), it returns a currency value such as $7.59. Do not use this method in a control that you use to enter data, because you would be creating a circular reference in which the function's argument must equal the field containing the function. This doesn't work.

Can I create controls on a form without creating associated labels?

Yes, you can set the AutoLabel default property for a type of control to No. Then Access does not add labels when you create a new control of that type. To view and change the default properties for controls, display the property sheet. Then click the tool for a type of control in the Toolbox. The property sheet lists the properties that apply to all controls of that type added to the active form or report. Figure 9-3 shows Access in the middle of setting the properties for new text boxes. The settings made here only change the text boxes you add to this form. This property sheet shows many properties you are familiar with as well as new ones like AutoLabel that you can only change for default controls.

Tech Note: If you want to change the default properties for all new forms or reports, you need to change the default properties for the form or report template.

Tech Tip: You can always delete the label part of a compound control. Select the label part of the compound control and press DEL. The rest of the compound control remains on the form or report design.

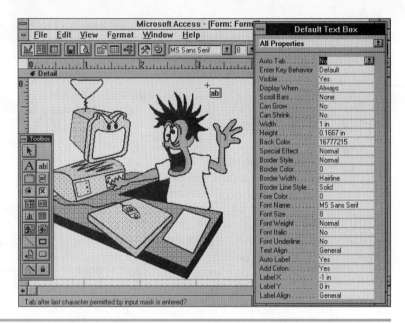

Back Color 16777215
Special Effect .... Normal
Border Style ...... Normal
Border Color 0
Border Width ..... Hairline
Border Line Style .. Solid

FIGURE 9-3 Property sheet showing settings for default text boxes

How do I remove lines created by a Report Wizard that I cannot find in the report's design?

Most of the lines added by a Report Wizard are at the bottom of a section. You can't see these lines because they are at the same location as the bottom of the section. The easiest way to remove them is to drag the bottom of the section down, select the line, press DEL, and return the section to its previous size. If the line isn't at the bottom of the section, choose a text box. Then keep pressing TAB to move through all the controls until you get to the line that you did not find. Press DEL.

My report has a calculated field. I want to get a total value, so I tried to sum this control, but I get a #Error. Why doesn't this work?

To sum the values from the calculated field, you need to reference the whole calculation. Access does not respond to summing a control name. Access appears to do this when it totals the fields from the table or query. However, in this case, the field names are the same as the names of the controls that display them. Access is really summing the field. Therefore, you need to enter the whole calculation as the Sum functions argument. For example, assume you have a control named Year_To_Date that has the ControlSource property = [Amount Owed] - [Amount Paid]. To get a total, you need to sum the whole expression as follows: = Sum([Amount Owed] - [Amount Paid]). This totals the calculation for all the records in your report.

Why does #Error appear in my text box when the source of data for the control is a formula that uses a field to supply one of the values?

The most likely reason for this error message is that the control has the same name as one of the fields you are using in its formula. Access thinks that the formula is referring to the control rather than to the field, creating a circular reference. For example, you might get this error if your text box's name is Unit Price and one of the fields you are using in the calculation is Unit Price. To fix this problem, change the name of the control.

How do I put a ceiling on the value entered into a field in my form?

You can specify a maximum value for a field with a ValidationRule property for that field's control. In the property sheet, type < and the ceiling value. For example, if a field should have a date before today's date, you can enter **<Date()** as the ValidationRule property. If you want users to enter a number less than 5,000, you can enter **<5000**.

Tech Tip: When you enter a validation rule, make sure the form's user knows what the appropriate limits are. Either add text next to the field describing the correct range, or include the correct range in the ValidationText property. Access displays a message box with the ValidationText property's contents when you try to leave the field and the validation rule is not met.

When I tab through my form, the order isn't from top to bottom. How can I fix it?

Access tabs through fields in the order in which you added them to the form. Therefore, if you add a new field to the top of a form, it is the last field in the tab order. To change the tab order:

1. Open the form in Design view.

2. Choose Ta**b** Order from the **E**dit menu. The Tab Order dialog box opens showing the current order.

3. Drag the fields in the Custom Order list box into the order you want to move between them.

4. Click OK to save your changes.

Tech Tip: You can quickly organize the tab order for controls from top to bottom again by selecting **A**uto Order in the Tab Order dialog box.

Why won't my report become narrower when I drag the right margin to the left?

The report has a control on the right side of the report. This control is preventing you from moving the margin. You cannot move a control by dragging the margin. You must move the control first, and then move the margin.

Tech Tip: To select the control that is causing the problem, click the horizontal ruler just to the left of the report's current margin. Clicking a ruler in Design view selects all controls below or to the right of the point you click.

My text displays extra data that I can't find in Design view. How do I remove the extra characters?

Most likely these extra characters are from a control you can't see because it's behind the text box. Check to see if anything, such as a label, lies behind the text box when in Design view. Click the text box and select Send to **B**ack from the F**o**rmat menu. If a control was behind the text box, you can now see it. At this point, you can select the control causing the problem and delete it.

How do I refer to my controls in my subforms and subreports?

The syntax for a control on a subform is

```
Forms![Form Name]![Subform Name].Form![Control Name]
```

The syntax for a control on a subreport is

```
Reports![Report Name]![Subreport Name].Report![Control Name]
```

For example, suppose you want to identify the Full Name control that appears on the Entering Names subform. The main form is Address Book. The correct syntax is

```
Forms![Address Book]![Entering Names].Form![Full Name]
```

If Entering Names and Address Book are both reports, you can enter

```
Reports![Address Book]![Entering Names].Report![Full Name]
```

A third possibility is that Address Book is a report and Entering Names is a subform (you cannot add a subreport control to a form). This entry is

```
Reports![Address Book]![Entering Names].Form![Full Name]
```

Tech Tip: The Expression Builder works well for entering the correct syntax for controls.

What syntax do I use to refer to controls on my sub-subforms?

You can extend the same syntax that you use to refer to a control to refer to a control in a subform that is in another subform. The syntax is

```
Forms![Form Name]![Subform Name].Form![Sub Subform
Name].Form![Control Name]
```

As an example, suppose you have a form named Overall. This form has a subform named Address Book. In the Address Book form is a subform control named Entering Names. The Entering Names form has a control named Full Name. To identify the Full Name control, you can use the syntax:

```
Forms![Overall]![Address Book].Form![Entering
Names].Form![Full Name]
```

Tech Tip: If one of the levels of the reference to the control is for a subreport, change the *Form!* in front of the report name to *Report!*. If the main object is a report rather than a form, replace *Forms!* with *Reports!*.

How can I attach a bitmap picture to my command button?

To display the contents of a bitmap graphic file on a command button, switch to the Design view of the form. View the properties for the command button, and move to the Picture property. Type the path name and filename of your bitmap image. For example enter **C:\WINDOWS\CARS.BMP** to display the image from this file on the command button.

Access copies the image from the bitmap file. The button has no link to the bitmap's file. You can also choose a bitmap image from the Control Wizard when you create your command button. In the last dialog box of the Wizard, select <u>B</u>rowse, and then select the picture.

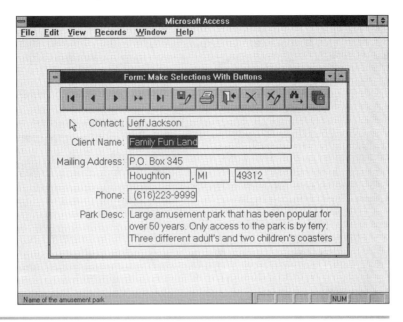

FIGURE 9-4   Command buttons using some of Access' built-in pictures

In addition, command buttons can display one of Access' built-in pictures. These pictures are available when you create the button with the Control Wizard. You can also choose one of these pictures by clicking the Build button at the end of the Picture property. The form in Figure 9-4 shows several of these pictures.

 **Tech Tip:**   Size and position the image in the file before you add it to the button. If you do not like how the picture looks on the button, you need to go back to the file and fix it there. Then you need to return to Access and select the bitmap picture again.

 ## How can I display information from another table on my form or report?

One way to do this is to use the DLookup function. DLookup returns the value of a field from any table. You can add this function as a calculated field to show a value from another table. DLookup uses three arguments: an expression, a domain, and

criteria. *Expression* is the name of the field containing the data you want to display. *Domain* is the name of a table or query, or an SQL statement that is the source of the data. *Criteria* selects which record or records this function uses. In this case, you probably want to compare a value in the table or query to something on your form or report.

As an example, suppose you have a form for a Payroll table that you use to enter weekly payroll information. When you use the form, you enter the employee's ID number. To make sure that you enter the correct number, this form has a calculated control that displays the employee's name from the Employee table. This calculated control's ControlSource property is

```
=DLookUp("[Employee]![First Name] & ' ' & [Employee]![Last
Name]","[Employee]","[Employee]![Employee Id] = Forms![Entering
Payroll]![Employee Id]")
```

This formula uses DLookup to return the first name and the last name from the Employee table and separates them with a space. You can see this in the form and its design shown here:

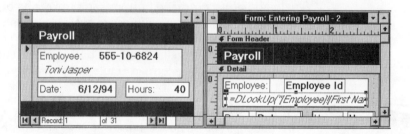

The other domain functions, such as DCount, DLast, DFirst, and DSum, work the same way. They use the same arguments, expression, domain, and criteria, but do different things with the selected data.

Tech Tip: DLookup only shows one field or expression at a time. If you want to display several fields or you want to edit the data from the other table, use a subform or subreport control instead.

Tech Terror: While the Expression Builder is great for adding control names and field names to domain aggregate functions like DLookup, it doesn't add the quotation marks. You will have to add them yourself.

 # Can I change the properties of all the controls of a specific type without having to select each one individually?

Yes, you can set the default properties for a control type and apply the defaults to other controls of that type. You have two ways to set the default properties for a control type:

- Select a control on the form and set its properties. Then choose Change Defaults from the Format menu.

- Display the property sheet and click the tool in the Toolbox for the control type you want to change. Make changes in the property sheet.

Either method sets the default for controls of that type. These defaults only affect controls added after setting the new defaults. However, you can apply these defaults to controls already on the form or report. Select the controls you want to use these defaults. Then choose Apply Defaults from the Format menu. The selected controls all acquire the default properties.

Tech Tip: You can also add buttons to the toolbar for the Apply Default or Change Default commands in the Format menu. These toolbar buttons are shown here, with the Apply Default button on the left and the Change Default button on the right.

Tech Terror: Changing a control back to the default settings for properties changes all of its properties. If you only want to change a few properties, select all the controls you want to change, and specify the new property setting. This way you leave the other property settings unchanged.

How can I give a default value to a calculated control?

You can't. If you think about it, you'll realize that you really don't want to. The whole reason for the calculated control is that it equals the value of a calculation.

How do I open a second form and have the same value appear on it as the value on the first form?

The event on the first form that triggers opening the second form needs a macro. This macro handles opening the second form and entering the value in a control. For example, you can have a form for entering invoices called New Order. When you enter a new customer name, you want to switch to your New Customer form to enter the information on the new customer, with the name that you typed already in place. The macro this first form contains has these actions:

- OpenForm to open the second form.
- GoToControl to move to the control on the second form whose value you want to set.
- SetValue to enter the value of the control on the second form.

A macro that performs this function might contain this information:

```
Action: OpenForm Arguments: Form Name:     New Customer
                            Data Mode:     Add
        GoToControl         Control Name: Customer Name
        SetValue            Item:         Forms![New Customer]!
                                          [Customer Name]
                            Expression:   Forms![New Order]!
                                          [Customer Name]
```

I've added a new record to the combo box, but it doesn't appear on my list when I pull it down. What's wrong?

All you need to do is refresh your screen. After you do this, the new item you added in the combo box will show up. To refresh the screen, choose <u>R</u>efresh from the <u>R</u>ecords menu.

Tech Tip: If you are adding other items to a combo box through a form, the form that adds the new items can refresh just the combo box control. An example of this appears in the question "Can I add values to a combo box or list box in the form I am working in?" later in this chapter.

Can I have a check box that sets a field to one of two values?

Setting a Yes/No field's value to one of two values is as simple as entering the field name for the ControlSource property of the check box control. However, to have a check box set the entry of another type of field:

1. Add a check box to the form.

2. Change the label attached to the check box control.

3. Write down the name of the check box control.

4. Add a text box control to the form.

5. Assign the text box control to the field with the value to assign.

6. Enter an IIF function in the ControlSource property of the text box that assigns the values depending on the check box status. An example might look like this:

```
= IIf([Priority], "Urgent", "Standard")
```

A check box's value is true when you select it and false when you clear it. The preceding example assigns Urgent to the field when the Priority check box is selected and Standard when it is not.

7. Change the text box's Visible property to No.

Now when you look at the form, you won't see the text box control, but it is invisibly setting the field's value depending on whether you select the check box.

I have a lot of single-character codes to enter. Can I get the form to move to the next field when I finish an entry?

To do this, use the InputMask and AutoTab properties. The InputMask property restricts the entry to just the number of characters set by the property. For example, you might enter **LL** as the input mask for a field containing state abbreviations, **00000-0000** for ZIP codes, or **A** for a field containing a single letter or number. Next set the AutoTab property for each of the code fields to Yes. When the AutoTab property is set to Yes, the focus automatically moves to the next control when the field is filled in.

Tech Tip: You can also have the InputMask property set the capitalization style. Type < to make the letters after this point lowercase and > to make them uppercase.

In Access 1.x, I had a list box and a text box that overlapped. The one that had the focus was on top. Why isn't this working anymore?

Access 2.0 has windowed and nonwindowed controls. List boxes and subforms are windowed. They are always on top. Other control types are nonwindowed. The one with the focus is on top of the others. You can also change their order by putting one in front or behind the other. If you have overlapping windowed controls, the one that is on top in Design view is on top in Form view.

How do I hide a form's control in the form's Datasheet view?

In Access 2.0, you must set the ColumnHidden property to True. Switch to the Datasheet view in the form's window. Select the column to hide, and then right-click it and choose Hide Columns. When you save the form's design, you also save the ColumnHidden property for the form's datasheet.

Can I set a Memo field's control so that the insertion point goes to the end of the entry when I move to the control?

When you move to a field's entry, initially the entire entry is selected. You can easily delete a long entry just by typing a character. If you want to deselect the entry and place the insertion point at the end of the entry, you can add a macro to the OnEnter property for the field. Use the SendKeys action to send F2, deselecting the entry. The insertion point then moves to the end of your data. The macro contains this information:

```
Action:   SendKeys   Arguments:   Keystrokes:   {F2}
                                   Wait:   No
```

This macro works for any type of field, not just Memo fields. If you want to be at the beginning of the field instead, replace {F2} with **{F2}^{HOME}**. ^{HOME} represents pressing CTRL+HOME.

Can I have page breaks in my report only when certain conditions are met?

Yes, you can add a page break control to a report and have this page break only work when certain conditions occur. The reason you can do this is that a page break control has a Visible property. When the page break's Visible property is Yes, the page break is in the report. When this control's Visible property is No, the page break is ignored.

This may seem strange to you, since you do not see a Visible property on the property sheet for a page break. Controls have some properties that you do not see on the property sheet. Usually these are the ones you use infrequently or only for programming. A page break's Visible property can be changed in a macro or in an Access Basic procedure. You can even add a condition for the macro's actions so that Access performs one action when the condition is true and another when the opposite condition is true. The macro uses two SetValue actions to change the Visible property.

For example, assume that in the Print Data report, you want a page break added when the Important Date field equals today's date. The page break control is named PageBreak37. The macro contains this information:

```
Condition: [Reports]![Print Data]![Important Date] = Date()
Action:    SetValue
Arguments: Item:  [Reports]![Print Data]![PageBreak37].[Visible]
           Expression:  Yes
Condition: [Reports]![Print Data]![Important Date]<>Date()
Action:    SetValue
Arguments: Item:  [Reports]![Print Data]![PageBreak37].[Visible]
           Expression:  No
```

Insert this macro as the OnFormat property of the Detail section. This macro makes sure that the page break only applies when the first condition is met and not when the second condition is met.

I have a calculated control that totals another calculated control in each group. Why isn't the RunningSum property working?

You need to modify your summary calculated control to make the RunningSum property work the way you want. Suppose you have a calculated control named Total and its ControlSource property is set to = Cost*Quantity. Instead of basing the second control on the calculated control, put the original calculation in the summary control's Control Source, as in = Cost*Quantity. Now you can use the RunningSum property in that control.

Can I add values to a combo box or list box in the form I am working in?

Yes, you can add new entries to a combo box or a list box while you work on the box's form. You do this by opening another form when you double-click the control. Assuming that you already have the combo or list box control and its form, follow these steps:

1. Create a form based on the same table or query that the combo or list box is based on. This is the form you use to add new records to appear in the combo or list box. As an example, if the list box lists the contents from the Gift Ideas table, create a form for adding records to the Gift Ideas table.

2. Create a new macro group. This macro group contains the following entries:

```
Macro Name:   AddNewRecord
Action:   OpenForm  Arguments:   Form Name:   Form to Add Records
                                 View:   Form
                                 Data Mode:   Add
                                 Window Mode:   Normal


Macro Name:   OnClose
Action:   DoMenuItem  Arguments:   Menu Bar:   Form
                                   Menu Name:   File
                                   Command:   Save Record
          SelectObject            Object Type:   Form
                                   Object Name:   Form With the
                                                  Box Control
                                   In Database
                                   Window:   No
          Requery                 Control Name:Control Name of
                                                Combo or List Box
```

3. Choose <u>C</u>onditions from the <u>V</u>iew menu and enter **[*First Field in Form*] Is Not Null** as the condition for the DoMenuItem action. This action will only save the current record if one is entered.

4. Switch to the form that you want the combo or list box to open.

5. Add the OnClose macro of the macro group you just created to this form's OnClose property. For example, if the macro group is named "Add Items to a List Box While in a Form," you will type **Add Items to a List Box While in a Form.OnClose** for the form's OnClose property.

6. Close this form that the control will open.

7. Open the form with the combo or list box in Design view and select the box's control.

8. Add the AddNewRecord macro of the macro group you created earlier to the control's OnDblClick property. For example, using the same macro group as in step 5, enter **Add Items to a List Box While in a Form.AddNewRecord**.

9. Switch to the Form view and double-click the list box.

This will open the other form on top, as you can see in Figure 9-5. At this point, you can enter new records and close the form. The first form will regain the focus. If you scroll through the list box, you will see your new entry.

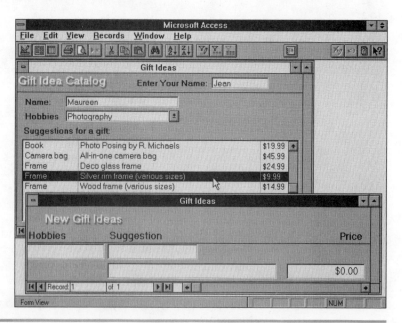

FIGURE 9-5   Having a list box open another form to add new entries

Can I refer to each column in a combo box separately?

Yes, you can build an expression that refers to separate columns of the selected row in a combo or list box. To refer to a particular column in the control, use the Column property of the combo box as in this example:

```
Forms![Form Name]![Combo Box Control Name].[Column](x)
```

X refers to the column number. For example, to refer to the second column from the Gift Idea Catalog form that you can see in Figure 9-5, the entry is = Forms![Gift Idea Catalog]![Suggested Gift].[Column](1). Notice how the column number is one less than the column number in the form. Access starts counting columns with 0, so the first column is column 0 and the second is column 1.

Tech Tip: A combo or list box can have columns that you can't see when that column has a width of 0. Do this when you want to refer to that value in another calculated field, but you don't want the value to appear in the combo or list box. However, when you are counting columns, you have to include all of them, including the ones you do not see.

How can I make small changes to the position or size of a control on a form?

First, select the control you want to adjust. To change the size of the field, press SHIFT and use the arrow keys to adjust the size. To move the control, press CTRL and use the arrow keys. You can also type measurements for the Top and Left properties to move the control to that location. Typing values for the Height and Width properties sets the size of the control.

Can I make a form that changes color as I tab through the fields?

Yes, you can. In the following form, the fields already selected are gray, the currently selected one is red, and the remaining ones are white.

To do the same to one of your forms:

1. Rename the fields by using a number. For instance, name the first field 1, the second field 2, and so on.

2. Create a macro group with the following information:

```
Macro Name:   ChangeToRed
Action:       SetValue
Arguments:    Item:        [Screen].[ActiveControl].[BackColor]
              Expression:  RGB(255,0,0)

Macro Name:   ChangeToGray
Action:       SetValue
Arguments:    Item:        [Screen].[ActiveControl].[BackColor]
              Expression:  RGB(130,130,130)

Macro Name:   First Control
Action:       GoToControl
Arguments:    Control Name:[1]
Action:       SetValue
Arguments:    Item:        [Forms]![Color Changer]![1].[BackColor]
              Expression:  RGB(255,0,0)
```

3. Switch back to the form.

4. Add the First Control macro to the OnEnter event property for the first control you select on the form.

5. Add the ChangeToRed macro to the OnEnter event property for the other controls you want to change color.

6. Add the ChangeToGray macro to the OnExit event property for all controls you want to change to gray when you move to another control.

7. Add an event procedure to the OnCurrent property of the form. It contains these instructions:

```
Sub Form_Current ()
Dim n As Integer
Dim s As String
For n = 1 To 3
    s = CStr(n)
    Forms![Color Changer](s).BackColor = RGB(255, 255, 255)
Next
DoCmd RepaintObject A_FORM, "Color Changer"
End Sub
```

This event procedure, named Color Changer, assumes that the form has three fields. If you have more than three fields, replace the 3 in the For n = 1 To 3 statement.

Now you have a data entry form that makes the current field red, the fields you have already been on gray, and fields you have not been on white.

How can I make a text box a specific color depending on the value of its data?

The BackColor of a text box is a property that you can change as you work on the form. The following example is a typical way of changing the color of a text box. Since this event procedure belongs to the form's OnCurrent property, you can add this code to the Categories form in the Northwind database to try it yourself. This procedure checks the current value of the Category Id field. If it is an even number, then it becomes light blue; if it is odd, it returns to white.

```
Sub Form_Current ()  ' Subroutine run on the current record
Original_Color = "16777215"
' Sets Original_Color equal to RGB value of white
If Me![Category Id] Mod 2 = 0 Then
' If Category Id is an even number then
    [Category Id].BackColor = "227727722"
    ' BackColor becomes "227727722"(light blue)
Else  ' Otherwise
    [Category Id].BackColor = Original_Color
    ' Category Id's BackColor becomes Original_Color
End If  ' End Condition Check
End Sub  ' End Subroutine
```

Sharing Data with Other Applications and Versions

One of the greatest advantages of Windows is that you can easily exchange data between different applications using the Windows Clipboard or OLE (Object Linking and Embedding) features. A simple cut-and-paste operation makes it easy to combine graphics, spreadsheet data, and text into a single attractive document. With OLE features, you can enter and format data in whatever application is the most suitable, and then use the data in any of your other applications. Access also shares data with other applications through importing, exporting, and attaching. These features are all designed so that you may easily reuse data without reentering it.

189

FRUSTRATION BUSTERS!

The easiest tool for exchanging data between applications is often overlooked—the Windows Clipboard. You can use the Clipboard to move and copy data not only within Access, but also to and from other applications. Whether you're cutting and pasting plain data, a fully formatted 3-D graph, or an OLE object, the Clipboard provides a quick, easy way to achieve your goal.

To copy Access data to a document in another application, simply cut or copy it from the Access datasheet. When you switch to the other application and paste the data, the columns and rows of data are placed in the application. Using the Clipboard is ideal when you want to insert a "snapshot" of your data in the other application, but keep in mind that once pasted, Access can't update that information.

You can also copy data from another application into Access. The data from other applications can be field entries or controls in a form or report design. You copy the data from the other application to the Windows Clipboard. Then paste it into your Access datasheet, form, or report. If the application that supplied the data does not support OLE, that data in Access is a simple copy. If that application does support OLE, that data in Access is an OLE object.

 I had to save Excel 5.0 worksheets as Excel 4.0 worksheets before I imported them into Access 1.x. Do I still have to do this?

No. Access 2.0 can import Excel 5.0 format files directly. To import an Excel 5.0 worksheet as an Access table:

1. Choose Import from the File menu.

2. Select Microsoft Excel 5.0 from the Data Source list box as the source of data to import.

3. Select the Excel worksheet to import and click the Import button.

4. Select the settings for importing the spreadsheet and select OK twice.

5. Select Close to finish importing.

Tech Tip: You can also directly export Access tables to an Excel 5.0 worksheet.

Does Access 2.0 use any new reserved words?

Yes, Access 2.0 now has many more reserved words. *Reserved words* are words that already have a special meaning to Access. They appear in Access Basic code or in SQL statements. Do not use these words as names for variables, objects, controls, or field names—errors may occur.

Access 2.0 has 28 new SQL reserved words, along with those that were already reserved in Access 1.*x*. Also, those marked with asterisks cannot be used in property settings or macro arguments. The new reserved SQL words are

All *	Double	Index	Outer	SmallInt	VarBinary
Any *	Exists *	Integer	Partial	Some *	VarChar
Counter	Foreign	Key	Percent	TimeStamp	YesNo
Database	Full	Match	Select *	Top	
Date	Ignore	OLEObject	Single	Values	

Access 2.0 also has Access Basic reserved words, which cannot be used as identifiers in code. The new Access Basic reserved words include

CompactDatabase	CreateUser	GoToPage	Parameter	RepairDatabase
Container	CreateWorkspace	Group	Property	Requery
CreateDatabase	CurrentUser	Idle	Quit	SetFocus
CreateField	Document	Index	Recalc	Set Option
CreateGroup	Echo	Indexes	Recordset	TableDef
CreateIndex	Field	InsertText	Refresh	TableDefs
CreateObject	Fields	Move	RefreshLink	Workspace
CreateProperty	FillCache	NewPassword	RegisterDatabase	
CreateRelation	GetObject	Object	Relation	
CreateTableDef	GetOption	OpenRecordset	Repaint	

How can I import an entire database?

You can import all of the objects from a closed Access database into the currently open one. To do this:

1. Choose Add-ins from the File menu while in the Database window.

2. Choose Import Database.

3. Specify the .MDB file that you want to import into your current database and select OK.

Access may ask a question or two along the way. When it is complete, you will see the message "Database successfully imported."

What does ODBC stand for?

ODBC stands for Open Database Connectivity. It is a powerful means of accessing data stored by a wide range of database management systems. Access uses ODBC drivers to manage information from different sources of data. The ODBC drivers that come with Access include ones for Access, FoxPro, dBASE, Paradox, and Btrieve. You may also have other ODBC drivers on your system that came with other applications.

What is an import/export specification?

Import/export specifications are the entries needed to either import or export delimited and fixed-width text files. For fixed-width text files, they precisely describe each field's name, data type, start point, and end point for any given record. For delimited text files, they describe the characters separating field entries and enclosing text entries. They contain the same information that you enter in the Import/Export Specification dialog box which opens when you choose Imp/Exp Setup from the File menu.

What is a fixed-width text file?

A *fixed-width* text file has fields of a fixed length. Figure 10-1 shows a fixed-width text file opened in the Notepad accessory. Each row, which is a single record, has the same fields. Each field is the same length in all records. In the fixed-width text file in Figure 10-1, each line contains a company name, phone number, city, date, and contact name. Each field uses a set number of positions, as shown here:

Field	Start Position	**Stop Position**	**Number of Columns**
Company name	1	20	20
Phone number	21	33	13
City	35	44	10
Date	45	53	9
Contact Name	54	78	25

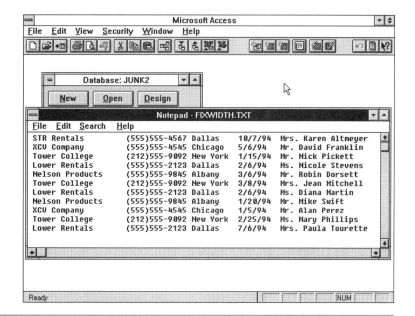

FIGURE 10-1   Fixed-width text file open in a Notepad accessory window

To import or export a file of this type, you need an import/export specification. To create one:

1. Choose Imp/Exp Setup from the File menu.

2. Select how dates in the text file appear in the Dates, Times, and Numbers section. You can choose the order of the date information, how date and time elements are separated, whether single-digit months and days have a leading 0, and whether years use four or two digits.

3. Enter field names, data types, starting points, and width in the Field Information list box. This is the most important part of the specification you are creating. The Field Name and Data Type columns are just like the ones you use to define fields in tables. The Start column indicates what column the field starts. The Width column entry indicates how many columns the field uses. The Field Information list box, shown here, displays the entries made for the specification to use when you import the FIXWIDTH.TXT file in Figure 10-1.

Field Information. (fixed width only)

Field Name	Data Type	Start	Width
Company Name	Text	1	20
Phone Number	Text	21	13
City	Text	35	10
Date	Date/Time	45	9
Contact Person	Text	54	25

4. Select OK when you finish entering the setup for how to import or export a text file.

5. Type a name for the specification in the Name text box in the Save Specification As dialog box. Your specification is now ready to use to import a fixed-width text file.

Tech Tip: The import/export specifications you save are saved as part of the current database. If you want to import the same fixed-width text file into another database, you have to reenter these specifications in that database.

Can I eliminate blank spaces between fields when I import a fixed-width text file?

Yes. When you import a fixed-width text file into a table in Access 2.0, you first need to define an import specification as described in the previous question. Normally, a field ends one position before the next one begins. However, this is not mandatory. If you know that your fixed-width text file has spaces that are always blank between some fields, you can define the import specifications to skip over the blank spaces. For example, the import specification shown in the following illustration assumes that there is a gap of five spaces between each field. The Full Name field occupies columns 1 through 25. The Address field doesn't start until column 31. The five spaces between the end of the Full Name field and the beginning of the Address field are simply ignored.

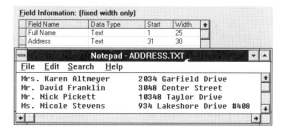

What formats can I "Output To" from the Database window's objects?

The Output To command in the File menu puts the contents of tables, queries, forms, reports, and modules in a file that other applications can open. The formats that your Access database objects can be output to are

- Microsoft Excel version 3.0 (*.XLS)
- Rich Text Format (*.RTF)
- MS-DOS Text (*.TXT)

To create one of these output files, choose Output To in the File menu. Then select the format you want for the file and select OK. Type the name for the file and select OK.

Access provides three toolbar buttons that can save a database object's results without your having to specify a format or a filename. These buttons are not initially available on any toolbar, but you can add them to the toolbars where you use their features. These buttons are

 Publish It with MS Word   Creates a rich text format file

 Analyze It with MS Excel   Creates an Excel worksheet

 Output to Notepad   Creates a text file

When you click one of these buttons, Access creates a file using a default filename, opens Word, Excel, or Notepad, and opens the file in that application.

Figure 10-2 shows an Access report after it has been saved in a file and then opened in Word for Windows. To open an Access report in Word for Windows, display the report in Access and click the Publish It with MS Word toolbar button.

Tech Tip: Access' Merge It button, shown here, starts a Wizard that guides you through creating a Word for Windows mail-merge document by using data from an Access table or query.

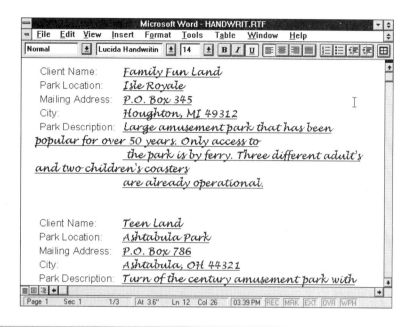

FIGURE 10-2   Access report put into a Word for Windows document

Tech Terror: The Publish It with MS Word, Analyze It with MS Excel, and Output to Notepad buttons have one drawback with forms and reports. These buttons will ignore any subforms, subreports, or graphs. If you use these buttons when working with a subform or subreport, Access will warn you that the data will be lost.

After I converted my Access 1.x database to Access 2.0, I get strange results when I open a form and look at a field I've called "Name." What's going on?

Your Name field probably is part of a calculation, and Access is confused about whether you mean the form's name or the field called Name. In Access 2.0, Name is a reserved word, which means it already has a special meaning. You need to rename this field in the table something other than "Name." For example, you can use Full Name, First Name, Name1, or some other variation. After you change the name for this field, everything will work fine.

To change a field name in a table:

1. Highlight the table in the Database window and click <u>D</u>esign.

2. Move to the line for the field you want to rename.

3. Replace the field name with the new one.

4. Select <u>S</u>ave from the <u>F</u>ile menu.

You will need to enter the field's new name in the other database objects that use the field. For example, every report that previously had a ControlSource property of Name needs to be changed.

Tech Tip: You may also be able to fix the form when Name is in a calculated field by replacing [Name] with [Form]![Name].

When I open my database, I see "Database *name* was created by a previous version of Microsoft Access. You won't be able to save changes made to object definitions in this database." How do I edit my database?

You see this error message because your database is still in the Access 1.*x* format. Some of the new Access 2.0 features can't be saved in the Access 1.*x* database format. You can still make changes to the data in tables without any problems. If you want to make full use of Access 2.0's features and avoid seeing this message again, you need to convert your database to the Access 2.0 format.

To convert your database:

1. Close any open database.

2. Choose Conver<u>t</u> Database from the <u>F</u>ile menu.

3. Select the database you want to convert and select OK.

4. Enter the name for the converted database and select OK.

Tech Terror: If you enter the same name twice, Access replaces your old database with the updated one. Unless you have a backup of your database, try to avoid doing this. If you run into any problems with the converted database, you can always go back to the old one.

Tech Tip: When you save your converted database with the name of the original database to replace the original, Access doesn't actually replace the old database until it's finished converting. You need to have enough space on your hard disk to hold two complete copies of your database for this to work.

In Access 1.*x* I used ANALYZER.MDA to print my table structure. How do I do this in Access 2.0?

In Access 2.0, you have two options to print the table structure or the definition of any other database object. The option you choose depends on whether you want to print the definition of a single object or the definitions of several objects. If you want to print the definition of a single object, choose Print Definition from the File menu, select the elements you want to print, and select OK.

If you want to document more than one object in the database, you can use the new Database Documentor to print a record of all of the tables or other objects in your database. To use the Database Documentor:

1. Choose Add-ins from the File menu, then choose Database Documentor.

2. Select the type of objects you want to document from the Object Type drop-down list box.

3. Double-click the object names you want to document.

4. Select Options, choose the information to print about the selected objects, and select OK.

5. Select OK to create the report.

6. Click the Print toolbar button to print the report and select OK.

7. Close the Report window when you are finished.

Print Definition in the File menu uses the Database Documentor without showing you all of the choices. If you want to save the data in the report, choose Save as Table from the File menu. This creates a table named Object Definition that contains some of the information you see in the report.

Why doesn't double-clicking objects with the right mouse button open objects in Design view?

In Access 2.0, right-clicking opens the shortcut menu for the object you clicked. To open the database object in Design view, press CTRL while double-clicking with the left mouse button.

Can I merge records from my tables into my word processor?

Yes, Access can provide data that your word processor can use as a merge data file. The method you use depends on which word processor you are using. To create a merge file that works with most word processors, create a query that selects the appropriate records. Select Export from the File menu, and export the query to a text file. Then you can use this text file as the merge file.

Another possibility is available when your word processor is Word for Windows. In this case, create a query to display the record or records you want in Word for Windows. Then you can put it into a rich text format file by choosing Output To in the File menu. Another possibility is to add the Merge It button to the toolbar and click it. This will start the Microsoft Word Mail Merge Wizard. This button already appears in the Database window toolbar. Figure 10-3 shows part of an Access table and the Word for Windows mail-merge document that uses this data. The Microsoft Word Mail Merge Wizard set up Word to use this Access data as the data source for the mail merge.

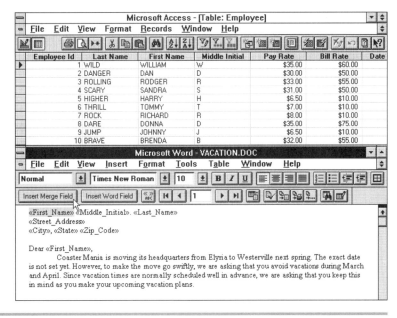

FIGURE 10-3 A Word for Windows mail-merge document that gets data from an Access table

Why do I get a compile error message or one that the Wizard cannot be found when I use a Wizard after converting my database from Access 1.*x* to 2.0?

In Access 2.0, whenever you run a Wizard, Access compiles all the modules in the database. This error message tells you that one of your modules contains incorrect syntax and cannot be compiled.

To pinpoint the problem, you need to compile each of your modules. Open one of the modules and click the Compile Loaded Modules toolbar button, or choose Compile Loaded Modules in the Run menu. When Access finds the problem, Access highlights the line of code that causes it. You can correct the offending line of code and then recompile the modules.

After fixing the error, you can run the Wizard without encountering this message.

After converting my database from Access 1.x to 2.0, I now see "To make changes to this field, first save the record" in the status bar when I try entering a new record by using a form. What's going on?

The form you are attempting to enter data with is based on an AutoLookup query. AutoLookup queries get information from two related tables. When you enter valid data in one field, the query enters related data from one of the tables into other fields. For example, when you enter an employee ID number, an AutoLookup query might get the mailing address for that employee from the Employee table, and enter it in the new record automatically. AutoLookup queries can make entering data easier and less error-prone. In this example, you can see from the other information displayed that you have entered the correct ID number.

You are having this problem because one of the fields filled in by the AutoLookup query has a DefaultValue property setting. Access is trying to enter this default value in the field, instead of using the looked-up value. To fix this problem, remove the DefaultValue property setting for all lookup fields.

Can I import dates formatted in a Year Month Day order?

Yes, you can import dates with a nonstandard format. When you import text files, you need to set the import specifications by choosing Imp/Exp Setup from the File menu. This command's dialog box has several options for setting the format of dates and times. Choose the order of the date elements from the Date Order drop-down list box. Access now knows that the dates in the text file you are importing use this order. It can then interpret the dates and translate them into its own date/time serial numbers correctly.

Which databases can Access import from and attach to?

Access can import and attach databases with the following formats:

- Paradox 3.*x*, 4.*x*
- FoxPro 2.0, 2.5, 2.6
- dBASE III, IV
- Btrieve
- SQL databases
- Other Access databases

Access can also import databases stored in the following formats, although these files cannot be attached as tables:

- Microsoft Excel 2.0-5.0
- Lotus 1-2-3 1.*x*-3.*x*
- Text (delimited)
- Text (fixed-width)

Tech Terror: You cannot attach Paradox 4.*x* tables until you change ParadoxNetStyle=3.x in the MSACC20.INI to ParadoxNetStyle=4.x and the Paradox NetPath entry to a directory containing a PDOXUSES.NET file.

Can I export only selected records from a table?

Yes, you can export selected records. However, you don't do it directly. To export selected records, you have to create a query containing only those records. You can then export the query. To do this:

1. Design a select query that displays only the records you want to export.
2. Save the query.
3. Choose Export from the File menu while in the Database window.
4. Choose a format from the Data Destination list box and select OK.
5. Choose the Queries option button, or select Queries from the Object Type drop-down list box.
6. Choose the select query from the Objects list box that selects the records you want to export.
7. Select OK and continue making selections that export the data you want. The remaining steps depend on the format you choose in step 4.

The resulting file contains all of the data you see in the select query.

Why are my attached SQL tables read-only, when I haven't specified them as such?

Attached SQL tables must have a unique index before you can edit them. Access requires that a unique index be defined for each table. SQL views and synonyms are also read-only when there is no unique index. To fix this problem, create a unique index for your table from your SQL server. Then reattach the tables to implement the changes.

How do I import a Lotus Notes file into Access 2.0?

To import a Lotus Notes file, export it from Lotus Notes to a Lotus 1-2-3 file. You can then import the Lotus 1-2-3 file into Access.

Can I use OLE to paste an Access table into another application, such as Word 6.0 or Excel 5.0?

No, Microsoft Access is not an OLE server; it is only an OLE client. This means that you can put data from other applications into Access, but you cannot put Access data into other applications. If you try to paste Access data into another application, the data is copied, not embedded or linked. This means that the pasted data has no continuing link with Access.

For example, when you paste an Access table into Word for Windows, the data appears as paragraphs with tabs separating each field or as a Word for Windows table. Figure 10-4 shows a Word for Windows table that contains data pasted from Access. Pasting an Access table into Excel copies the data in the table in the same column-and-row format that you see in a Datasheet view. This data appears in these applications just as if you had entered it there.

Invoice Number	Invoice Date	Invoice Amount	Client Name	Coaster Name
1062	10/31/93	$1,200,000	Amusement Technologies	Scream Machine
1078	4/1/94	$1,700,000	Amusement Technologies	Scream Machine
1092	6/1/94	$600,000	Amusement Technologies	Scream Machine
1021	12/31/92	$250,000	Amusement Technologies	Astro Transport
1058	7/30/93	$2,750,000	Amusement Technologies	Astro Transport
1063	10/31/93	$3,000,000	Amusement Technologies	Astro Transport
2005	7/1/94	$1,800,000	Amusement Technologies	Astro Transport
1057	6/30/93	$500,000	Amusement Technologies	Scream Machine
1093	6/1/94	$198,000	Arden Entertainment Group	Taurus
1085	5/1/94	$1,150,000	Family Amusements	Corker
1070	1/31/94	$350,000	Family Amusements	Corker
1074	3/1/94	$1,600,000	Family Fun Land	Red Dragon
1071	1/31/94	$300,000	Family Fun Land	Red Dragon
1068	1/31/94	$400,000	Family Fun Land	Red Dragon
1072	3/1/94	$200,000	Family Fun Land	Red Dragon
1005	3/30/92	$1,500,000	Island Waterplay Inc.	White Lightnin
1018	10/31/92	$1,100,000	Island Waterplay Inc.	White Lightnin
1056	6/30/93	$500,000	Island Waterplay Inc.	White Lightnin
1030	3/31/93	$400,000	Playland Consortium	Wild One
1059	8/30/93	$1,000,000	Playland Consortium	Wild One
2006	7/1/94	$1,800,000	Playland Consortium	Wild One
1012	6/30/92	$200,900	Teen Land	The Runaway

FIGURE 10-4   Access table data pasted into a Word for Windows table

In Access 1.x, one of my tables used the User() function to check for a valid user. This isn't working now that I upgraded to Access 2.0. How can I get this to work?

The User() function cannot be used in tables in Access 2.0. Instead, check for a valid user from a form with the CurrentUser() function. For example, the field's control in the form can have its BeforeUpdate property assigned to run a macro. This macro tests that the CurrentUser() function result did not match an entry. If this condition test is true, the macro can perform the CancelEvent action to abandon the BeforeUpdate event and prevent changes by an unauthorized user.

How do I create OLE links now that I don't have Paste Link in the Edit menu?

The command for pasting OLE links has changed. In Access 1.x, you created an OLE link with the Paste Link command in the Edit menu. To create an OLE link in Access 2.0:

1. Choose Paste Special from the Edit menu.
2. Select the Paste Link option button.
3. Select OK.

 ## Can an append query add records to a FoxPro or Paradox database?

Yes. An append query can transfer records to other tables, even if the destination table is a dBASE, FoxPro, or Paradox database. The dBASE, FoxPro, or Paradox database doesn't even have to be attached to an Access database, though it does need to use a unique index. To modify a query to do this:

1. Choose Append from the Query menu, or click the Append Query toolbar button.

2. Type the name of the database after Table Name in the Query Properties dialog box.

3. Select the Another Database button.

4. Type the path of the other database file in the File Name text box.

5. Type a space, a quotation mark, the source for the data, a semicolon, and another quotation mark after the path in the File Name text box. The source of the data is the same text that you see in the Data Source list box displayed by choosing Attach Table in the File menu. An example of the complete entry for appending data to a Paradox 4.0 database is C:\PARADOX "Paradox 4.x;".

6. Select OK.

7. Enter the fields to append to in the Append To row of the QBE grid.

8. Select Run from the Query menu, or click the Run button in the toolbar.

9. Select OK twice to confirm that you want to append the data and to confirm the number of records you are appending.

When I try attaching a Microsoft SQL Server table, I get the message "Reserved error 7745; there is no message for this error." What does this mean?

This message appears because the Microsoft SQL server is not communicating with the ODBC driver, a file Access uses to work with databases created by other database management programs. Run the INSTCAT.SQL script with your Microsoft SQL server to prepare it for communication with the ODBC driver.

Access Setup does not automatically install the INSTCAT.SQL script. Before running it, you need to decompress the file on the Access Setup Disk 1 and copy it to your hard drive. Use DECOMP.EXE, on the same disk, to decompress the file. Switch to the DOS prompt, and then enter **A:\DECOMP.EXE A:\INSTCAT.SQ_ C:\INSTCAT.SQL**. This copies and decompresses the INSTCAT.SQ_ file to INSTCAT.SQL on drive C. Specify different drives or directories as needed.

Why does Access not lock records in my attached SQL table when I have record locking set?

When you work on an attached SQL table, the SQL database controls the locking. Therefore, the locking does not change, regardless of what your setting is in Access. Access always acts as if this is set to No Locks. To change how the records are locked, change them from the SQL database.

How can I bring my text file into Access when the fields are delimited with semicolons, records are separated with carriage returns/line feeds, and each record has a different number of fields?

You have several options for bringing delimited data into Access. You can import a delimited text file by choosing Import from the File menu from a Database window and selecting how fields and records are separated. To import delimited data in a macro, you use the TransferText action. In an Access Basic procedure, you use DoCmd TransferText.

However, none of these options works if the number of fields varies for each record. Instead, use the Input function within an Access Basic procedure to import this type of input. The procedure must perform several steps to evaluate the incoming data. The procedure will read each character and process for the end of the file, the end of the line, and for the location of semicolons. The Input function can read the file character-by-character into a string until it finds a semicolon. When it finds a semicolon, the code tests the data to determine which field that data belongs to. To do this, use functions such as VarType(), IsDate(), or IsNumeric() to determine which type of data the string contains, and to decide which field the string represents according to its data type. The code continues to read characters until the Input function reaches the end of the record. Then the code enters the record in the appropriate table. The steps of reading characters from the line, dividing strings into fields, and deciding which fields they represent are repeated until the end of the file is reached.

How do I set up Access to attach to Btrieve tables that I attached with Access 1.1?

If Btrieve isn't in the list of sources for importing and attaching data, the Btrieve ISAM driver isn't installed for Access 2.0. ISAM drivers provide settings that affect how Access writes and reads data. If you look at the MSACC20.INI file, it is missing a Btrieve section. To add this ISAM driver:

1. Select the MS Access Setup icon from the Program Manager.

2. Select the Add/Remove button to add that component.

3. Select the ISAM Drivers check box.

4. Select the Change Option button.

5. Select Btrieve ISAM and OK.

6. Select Continue to install the drivers and update the proper files. Now you will be able to access Btrieve tables.

 Why does my Paintbrush picture look incorrect when I insert it into Access as an OLE object?

The picture may need its scaling changed. Switch to the form or report design, and select the control that displays the OLE object. Open the property sheet and select the SizeMode property. You probably want to select *Zoom* to make the picture as large as possible without distorting it. Your other choices are *Stretch,* which fills the object with the picture even if it has to change the height-to-width ratio, and *Clip,* which shows the picture at its original size even if the control is too small and can only show the upper-left corner.

If that doesn't fix the problem, insert the picture from a file. As an example, suppose you want to add the picture in LOGO.BMP to a form design or as an object in an OLE Object data type field in a form or datasheet. To do this:

1. Choose Insert Object from the Edit menu.

2. Choose Create from the File menu.

3. Choose Browse to open a Browse dialog box so you can select the file to insert.

4. Select the name of your .BMP file and click OK. This picture will look the same as it did in Paintbrush.

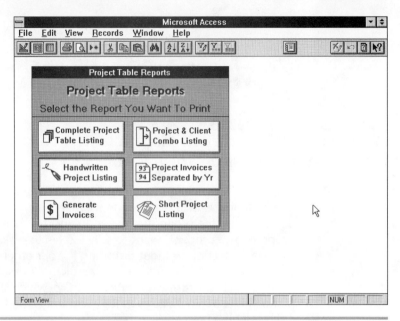

FIGURE 10-5   Paintbrush files inserted into an Access form

Figure 10-5 shows several Paintbrush files inserted into an Access form as the pictures for the command buttons.

How do I import a .DIF file into Access?

To import a .DIF file, you have to use another application as an intermediate step. This other application needs to be able to import a .DIF file and then save it in one of the file formats Access can import. The following series of steps uses Excel as the intermediate application. To do this:

1. Open Excel.

2. Choose <u>O</u>pen from the <u>F</u>ile menu.

3. Select Data Interchange Format (*.dif) from the List Files of <u>T</u>ype drop-down list box.

4. Select the file to import into Excel in the File <u>N</u>ame list box and select OK.

5. Choose Save <u>A</u>s from the <u>F</u>ile menu.

6. Select Microsoft Excel Workbook from the List Files of Type drop-down list box. If you are using an earlier version of Excel, the choice you make is the default selection for Excel worksheet files.

7. Type a name for the new file and select OK.

8. Open Access and the database to contain the data from the .DIF file.

9. Choose Import from the File menu.

10. Choose Microsoft Excel 5.0 or Microsoft Excel 2.0-4.0 below Data Source and select OK.

11. Select the Excel file and Import.

12. Select Close.

Built-in Functions and Macros

Built-in functions and macros affect almost everything you create in Access. They are productivity tools that provide values and perform actions.

Built-in functions provide ready-to-use formulas. You can use them in queries to create calculated fields. They can display values on forms and reports, or set property values. Macros and modules also use built-in functions. In the next chapter, you will learn about Function procedures, so you can create additional functions to use along with the ones Access provides.

Macros perform a series of actions. These actions are similar to menu commands and other selections you make as you work with a form or report. They can guide you through entering data and working with forms and reports. Macros may not be as comprehensive as Access Basic procedures, which provide full programming capabilities, but they are wonderful for shorter tasks.

In other chapters, you have seen functions and macros at work. This chapter focuses on questions that are specific to functions and macros, rather than the questions that are answered by using functions and macros. If you already have used other packages, you are probably familiar with using functions. Macros are a less familiar feature. To help you get started, some of the basic terms you'll need to know for working with macros are described in the following Frustration Busters box.

FRUSTRATION BUSTERS!

A macro uses some terms you may not recognize. To get the most out of this chapter's tips on macros, you need to understand these terms.

- *Action*—A macro command that describes something you want the macro to do.

- *Condition*—A logical statement next to an action that determines whether the action is performed. When the condition is true, the action next to it is performed. Otherwise, the action is ignored. Enter conditions in the Condition column next to the macro actions to provide control over the performance of an action. Enter **...** in the Condition column when you want the condition that applied to the previous action to also apply to the action in the row with the three dots.

- *Macro*—A set of actions to perform. Macros are stored either as individual database objects or as part of a macro group that is a database object.

- *Macro Group*—A collection of macros stored as a single database object. Name macros within a macro group by displaying the Macro Name column and entering the name in this column. Only the first action in a macro needs a name. All of the other actions after the name and before the next one are part of that macro. To identify a macro in a macro group, enter the macro group name, a period, and the name of the macro.

Why isn't the control that shows the result of = ("Date") displaying the current date?

The correct syntax of the Date function is = Date(). = Time() returns the current time. You can also enter = Now() if you want both the date and time.

When using a function, always put the parentheses after the function's name. If the function requires any arguments, place them inside the parentheses. Do not place quotations around the function name. The general syntax is

```
FunctionName(Argument1, Argument2, ..., ArgumentN)
```

Tech Tip: If you are having problems remembering the syntax for a function, add and edit the function with the Expression Builder. When you add a function with the Expression Builder, your entry contains both the function and placeholders for all of the function's arguments. It makes sure that you don't forget a closing parenthesis.

How can I test for multiple criteria or situations in a query, form, or report with the IIf function?

You can test for multiple conditions in an IIf function by including another IIf statement as the true or false argument of the first IIf function. This is called *nesting* because one function is nested within another. Nesting uses the result of one function as the argument for another. An example is

```
IIf([Field A]=1,IIf([Field B]=2,IIf([Field C]=3,"Three","Not
Three"),"Not Two"),"Not One")
```

Tech Tip: In a Function or Sub procedure, use If ... Then ... Else instead. It performs faster.

This example first tests whether the value of Field A is 1. When the value of this field is not 1, this expression returns the entry "Not One." Otherwise, Access evaluates the true part of the first IIf function, which is another IIf function.

In the second IIf function, Access tests whether the value of Field B is 2. Depending on whether the value for Field B equals 2, this function either returns the string "Not Two," or it evaluates the third IIf function. You can continue nesting for as many layers as necessary.

When I use a Val function in an IIf function, the IIf function returns my numbers as text instead of integers. How do I fix this?

Make sure that the true part and false part of the IIf function are numeric. You are probably using the IIf function to return one of two expressions as a calculated field. For example, IIf(Field1 = "OH", 1, Val([Field0])) returns a 1 or the value in Field0. On the other hand, when the true part and false part are different data types as in IIf(Field1 = "OH", "", Val([Field0])), the values returned by the Val function are treated as text in the query's datasheet. This can change how records are ordered if you use the calculated field for sorting.

What is a domain function?

A domain function performs a calculation, such as a sum or average, on a field of a subset of the records in a query or table. Some common domain functions include DLookup, DSum, DCount, DFirst, DLast, and DAvg. All of these functions have the same syntax, *FunctionName*(Expression, Domain, Criteria). *Expression* is the field name you want evaluated. *Domain* is the table or query that contains the field to evaluate. *Criteria* is an expression that is evaluated according to the records, and only the records that meet the criteria are included in the calculation. As an example, you might have the following function:

```
DCount("[Customer Name]","Customer","[State]='OH'")
```

This function counts the number of customer names in the Customer table for only the records where the State field contains OH.

Why is the DLookup function returning "#Name?" or "#Error"?

Generally, the #Name? error occurs when you incorrectly enter the function. Common mistakes include not putting = (equal sign) before the function name in the ControlSource property, forgetting the quotes around one of the arguments, or mistyping the function name. #Error generally occurs when you mistype either the table or query name (the domain) or the name of a field within this function.

In Access 1.1, I set a variable to the current database by using CurrentDB(). How do I do this in Access 2.0?

To set a variable to the current database in Access 2.0, use the syntax *variablename* = DBEngine(0)(0) or *variablename* = DBEngine.Workspaces(0).Databases(0). The first (0) selects the Workspaces collection. The second selects the Database collection.

Another way to assign the database name to the variable name is with this code:

```
Dim MyDB As Database
Set MyDB = DBEngine.Workspaces(0).Databases(0)
variable = MyDB.Name.Value
```

What is a macro?

A macro is a list of tasks that Access will carry out for you. These tasks include opening and closing forms, printing reports, and setting the values of controls on a form. Figure 11-1 shows a Macro window that contains macros saved in a macro group. Their names appear in the Macro Name column just before the macro's first action. When a Macro window only contains one macro, rather than a macro group, the Macro Name column is empty and can be hidden. The optional Condition column has any conditions that determine whether to perform the action to the right. The Action column contains the instructions to perform. As you move between rows in the top half of the window, the bottom half of the window shows the arguments for the action.

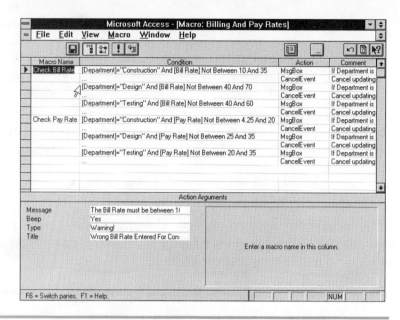

FIGURE 11-1 Macros saved in a macro group

 How many macro actions can I have in one macro?

Your macros may have as many as 999 actions. This limit applies to the contents of a Macro window, so macros within a macro group are limited to 999 actions for the entire group.

 How can a macro display a message when a user enters an item in a combo box that is not in its list box?

To execute a macro when a user enters a new item in a combo box, you need to:

- Enter the macro name for the combo box's OnNotInList property.

- Set the LimitToList property to Yes.

Once these two things are done, the macro will execute. The NotInList event occurs when a value is entered in the combo box that does not appear on its list while the LimitToList property is set to Yes.

Tech Tip: The MsgBox action displays messages. The arguments for this action supply the message to display, determine whether the computer beeps, select the icon in front of the message, and specify the text that appears at the top of the message's dialog box.

How do I tell my macro to move the focus to a control on a subform?

The GoToControl action moves the focus to a control, such as a subform control. This action only accepts one control name and *not* the full reference syntax of a control on a subform. You cannot use Forms![*Main form*]![*Control Name Of Subform*].Form![*Control On Subform*] as a Control Name argument for the GoToControl action. However, subforms are considered just another control on an Access form. Therefore, add the following actions to your macro:

- A GoToControl action, and specify the control name of the subform as the Control Name argument.

- Another GoToControl action. This time, put the control name of the control within the subform as the Control Name argument.

If there's another layer to this scenario, as in a subform within a subform, just add one more GoToControl action.

How many characters can I have in a comment of a macro?

You can enter as many as 255 characters in a macro's comment. Comments are where you describe the purpose of each action.

My AutoExec macro displays an opening screen for my application. Can I prevent this screen displaying every time I open my database?

To keep an AutoExec macro from executing when you open the database, press SHIFT while you select the database to open.

In a macro that updates a table, can I prevent the message "Updating X records..." from appearing?

Yes, add the SetWarnings action to the macro. The default for this action is No. This action prevents showing system messages such as updating records and appending records. Access still displays error messages.

Is there a length limit for macro conditions?

A macro's condition can be up to 255 characters. If your condition is longer than this, use an Access Basic procedure instead.

Can a macro make sure that a value entered in a form already exists in a table's field?

Yes, a macro can limit entries to a predefined list of options stored in a field. You do this by placing a condition in front of the macro's actions that tests whether the value is acceptable. When this condition is true, Access performs the actions that handle the new entry. When this condition is false, Access skips over the macro actions. The condition uses the DCount domain aggregate function to test whether the field has a matching entry. To add this condition:

1. Create the macro and add the actions that you want performed when the form entry *does not* match any existing entry in a table's field. For example, adding a CancelEvent action stops the updating process. This action combined with the condition lets you halt the updating unless the entry has a match in the field.

2. Click the Conditions toolbar button shown here, or choose <u>C</u>onditions from the <u>V</u>iew menu to add the Condition column to the Macro window.

3. Move to the Conditions column in the row containing the first macro action.

4. Enter the following condition:

```
DCount("[Field In Table]","Name Of Table","[Match Field in
Table]=Forms![Form Name]![Control On Form])=0
```

In this condition, *Field In Table* is the field name from the table to count entries. *Name Of Table* is the table name containing the entry to match. *Match Field in Table* is the name of the field to match from the table. *Form Name* and *Control on Form* identify the form and control with the entry you are testing. This function returns the number of matching entries it finds from the table. If DCount cannot find a matching entry, this function equals 0. This makes the condition true, so Access performs the action next to the condition. You can change the =0 to >0 for conditions used with actions you want performed when Access *does* find a matching entry.

5. Type **...** below this condition to repeat it for the other actions that are performed depending on whether the DCount function finds a matching entry.

6. Save the macro.

7. Attach the macro to the event you want to trigger the macro.

8. Use the form. When you make an entry and the event that triggers the macro occurs, Access tests the value you have entered as the condition for the macro entry.

As an example, suppose you want a form's BeforeUpdate event to run a macro that rejects an entry in the form's FirstName control when it does not match any existing entry in the FirstName field in the Friends table. You would attach a macro to the OnBeforeUpdate property that has a CancelEvent action and the following condition:

```
DCount("[FirstName]","Friends","[FirstName] = Forms![Form1]!
[FirstName]")=0
```

How does a macro refer to a control in a subform?

Macros frequently need to reference a specific control in a form. The syntax for a reference to a control that is part of a subform control is Forms![*Main Form Name*]![*Sub Form Name*].Form![*Sub Control Name*]. For example, to identify the Hours control in the Billed Hours subform control in the Invoice Generation form (shown in Figure 11-2), you would enter:

```
Forms![Invoice Generation]![Billed Hours].Form![Hours]
```

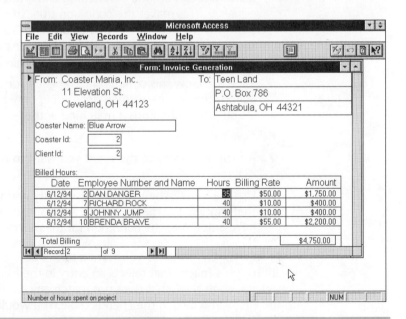

FIGURE 11-2   Form containing a subform

How does a macro move the focus from a control on a subform to a control on the main form?

When a macro needs to move the focus from a control on a subform to a control on a form, it needs the SelectObject and GoToControl actions. The actions and their arguments are

```
Action:  SelectObject  Arguments:  Object Type:  Form
                                    Object Name:  Form Name
                                    In Database Window:  No
Action:  GoToControl   Arguments:  Control Name:  Control Name
                                                  in Form
```

For example, suppose you want to move the focus from the Hours control in the Billed Hours subform in Figure 11-2 to the Coaster Name control in the Invoice Generation form. The SelectObject action has an Object Name argument of Invoice Generation. The GoToControl action has a Control Name argument of Coaster Name.

How can I have a macro temporarily ignore a line while I test the macro?

You can disable any line by putting a condition in front of it that is always false. Choose Conditions from the View menu, or click the Conditions button on the toolbar. Type **0** into the condition for the lines you want to ignore. An action only executes if the condition evaluates as true. The 0, which is what false equals, prevents the macro from executing that particular line. Remember that this affects *only* the line to which you added the 0. When you no longer want this line ignored, remove the 0.

How can a macro import dBASE files?

What your macro needs is one of the three Transfer macro actions: TransferText, TransferSpreadsheet, or TransferDatabase. These macro actions can import or export files. In the case of TransferDatabase, the macro can attach the table to the database. Let's look at the TransferDatabase macro. This macro has seven arguments.

- *Transfer Type* determines whether you want to import, export, or attach a database table.

- *Database Type* sets the format of database that the action will work with, such as Paradox, dBASE, or FoxPro.

- *Database Name* is a little tricky:

  - When the macro will import, attach, or export an Access database, enter the full path name, including the filename of the database.

  - When the macro will import, attach, or export to a database format that stores tables in individual files, you only need to enter the path to the directory where the file is kept.

- *Object Type* only applies when the object the macro will import, attach, or export is part of an Access database. Choose Table, Query, Form, Report, Macro, or Module for the type of object. When the Database Type is not Microsoft Access, you can ignore this argument. The other database types only operate with table objects, so this action ignores the Object Type argument.

- *Source* is the actual name of the object you are using.

  - For Access objects, enter the name of the database object as it appears in the Database window.

  - For other database types, enter the filename without the file extension.

- *Destination* is similar to Source, except it refers to the name you want to give the new object. When you export to something other than an Access database, you must enter a valid filename without an extension. Otherwise, enter a database object name valid within an Access database.

- *Structure Only* applies when the Database Type is Microsoft Access and the Object Type is Table. In all other cases, the action ignores this argument's entry. Enter **Yes** when the macro will import or export an Access table and you want just the structure, or definition, of a table—without the data.

The following macro imports a dBASE file called MEMBER.DBF located in the DBASE directory. In the Access database, this imported table is named New Test.

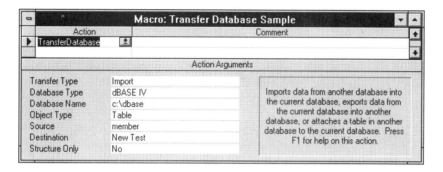

Can a macro import or export a text file?

The TransferText macro action imports or exports a text file. It is just like the TransferDatabase macro action described in the previous question. However, you also need to include a specification name for how the text is separated into fields and whether the first row contains field names.

How can I create a custom menu bar with macros?

Forms and reports have a MenuBar property. This property runs a macro that sets the menu that appears when you use the form or report. To create this menu bar, simply attach a macro that performs AddMenu actions to the MenuBar property. The macro you attach uses several AddMenu actions. These actions specify the individual menu names. They also call macros to execute when menu commands are selected.

As an example, a macro to make Close a menu bar selection includes the AddMenu action. Its arguments include

- *Menu Name: &Close* This is the selection on the menu bar. The C is underlined because of the ampersand (&) in front of it.

- *Menu Macro Name: CloseMacro*   This is the name of the macro to perform when you select <u>C</u>lose.

- *Status Bar Text: Closes the Form*   This is the text that displays in the status bar when you highlight the menu bar selection.

This macro is named NewMenu. This macro needs another macro, CloseMacro, which actually performs the action of closing the form. CloseMacro contains a Close action with Form as the Object Type argument and the form's name as the Object Name argument.

The final step would be to enter the NewMenu macro for the MenuBar property of the form. When the form is opened, the custom menu bar displays with only the <u>C</u>lose option.

The menu system for forms or reports is an all-or-nothing proposition. When you have a macro for the MenuBar property, the menu the macro creates entirely replaces the existing menu. All of the standard menu bar disappears, unless you add it as part of the MenuBar property's macro. This is why you are better off creating a menu with the Menu Builder add-in when you only want a few changes. This add-in creates macros that set up most of the existing menu, letting you focus on what you want to change. Figure 11-3 shows part of the New MenuBar macro that creates the new menu bar, and the New Menubar_File macro, which creates the <u>F</u>ile menu for this menu bar. You can see in Figure 11-3 that this custom menu bar has fewer options than the default.

To start the Menu Builder:

1. Select Add-<u>i</u>ns from the <u>F</u>ile menu, and then select <u>M</u>enu Builder.

2. Select the macro containing the menu to edit, and then select <u>E</u>dit to work with existing menus. You can select <u>N</u>ew to create a new menu, and then select an Access menu on which to base it. You will see a Menu Builder dialog box like the one in Figure 11-4.

3. Make changes to the menu such as:

- *Modify an item*   Move to the item in the list and change the contents of the Ca<u>p</u>tion, <u>A</u>ction, Arg<u>u</u>ment(s), and Status Bar <u>T</u>ext text boxes.

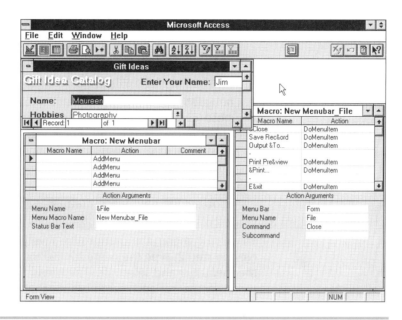

FIGURE 11-3   Macros that create a menu

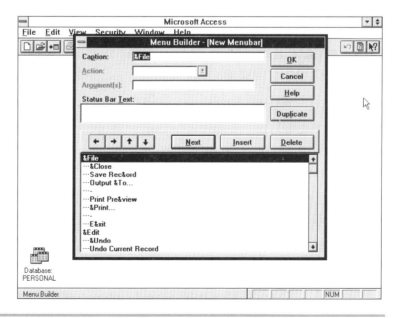

FIGURE 11-4   Menu Builder for modifying a menu system with macros

- *Delete an item*   Move to the item in the list and select Delete.

- *Move a menu item around in a menu*   Highlight the item to move in the list, and click the up or down arrow.

- *Change the menu level of an item*   Move to the item whose level you want to change and click the left or right arrow.

- *Add a menu item*   Move to the menu item in the current list below where you want the new item added. Select Insert. Make entries in the Caption, Action, Argument(s), and Status Bar Text text boxes.

4. Select OK when the menu is completed. If you are editing an existing menu, the changes are saved. If you selected New in step 2, type the name for the macro that creates the menu bar and select OK. The Menu Builder creates the other macros and macro groups that will display the menu you have designed.

At this point, your menu is ready. To use it, enter the name of the macro you selected in step 2 or typed in step 4 as the MenuBar property for a form or report.

Can I create a custom menu that is only available when certain conditions exist?

Yes, you can create a menu available when specific conditions exist. Custom menus are created with macros that you can add to a form or report. You can add conditions in front of the AddMenu actions in the macro to determine whether the menu is available.

I want to open my custom menus using ALT and an underlined letter, the same way I can use ALT+F to open the File menu. How can I do this?

To underline a letter in your custom menu's title, place an ampersand (&) in front of the letter to underline. When the menu appears on the menu bar, the letter following the ampersand is underlined. You can press ALT+*the underlined letter* to open the menu. You can also add ampersands to underline letters for commands that appear in one of the menus.

When creating custom menus, how can I add a line separating options in the menu?

When you are in the Menu Builder, move to where you want the line and add a menu item. For this menu item, type - in the Caption text box. Access handles displaying the rest of the line when you display the menu. This provides the same feature as entering a hyphen (-) repeatedly for the menu name as required in Access 1.*x*.

Access Basic Programming

Access Basic is Access' programming language. Blocks of Access Basic code are saved as procedures in modules. You can run these procedures separately or as part of other database objects. The following Frustration Busters box provides definitions of the Access Basic building blocks.

FRUSTRATION BUSTERS!

The following terms are used in Access Basic code:

- *Collections* are groups of the same type of objects, such as a group of tables.

- *Comments* are text within a procedure that Access does not execute as Access Basic code. They often describe the code in a procedure. Comments start with an ' (apostrophe), and can appear on their own line or at the end of a line of Access Basic code.

- *Constants* store fixed information. Their value never changes.

- *Events* are any action that will trigger execution of a procedure—such as closing a form or saving a record.

- *Methods* are *statements* or functions that belong to specific objects.

- *Objects* are references to things in your database such as forms, or things within database objects such as controls on a form.

- *Statements* are Access Basic instructions.

- *Variables* store information that changes while a procedure executes. You can assign variables a value or have Access assign a value based on data in your database. Variables in Access Basic, unlike in other languages, can store entire objects such as tables. Variables follow Access Basic naming rules.

Names in Access Basic can be up to 40 characters long, including letters, numbers, and underscores (_). They must start with a letter. You cannot use some words, called *reserved words*, as names in Access Basic. Access Basic already uses reserved words for specific meanings. For example, "Null" is a reserved word that refers to fields without entries.

What is a module?

Modules contain Access Basic code. Each module has a declarations section that stores information available to all of the procedures in that module. This information includes user-defined data types, global constants, global variables, and references to external procedures in a dynamic link library (DLL). The rest of the module is filled with Function and Sub procedures. You can store all of your Access Basic code in one module or in several different ones.

Forms and reports can have their own module to store the procedures used in that form or report. This module gathers all the procedures for a form or report into one location. However, a form or report can also perform procedures that are in a separate module.

I have trouble with syntax in Access Basic. Is there an easy way to write code?

Access' online help is a great source for finding correct syntax. First, search the online help for the command, method, or action you want to use. You can select the <u>S</u>earch button in the Help application's toolbar. Once you display the help topic about that command, method, or action, click Example or Access Basic under the topic heading. Help displays an example of Access Basic code like the one shown in Figure 12-1. Select Copy from the toolbar to place the sample Access Basic code on Windows' Clipboard. Then select Paste to add the sample code to your database. Remember to change the arguments of the pasted code to reflect your actual database.

Tech Tip: You can copy code from one procedure to another with the Clipboard. Select the code to copy by dragging the mouse across it. Then right-click the mouse and choose Copy. Next, switch to where you want the code, right-click where you want the code added to the procedure, and choose Paste.

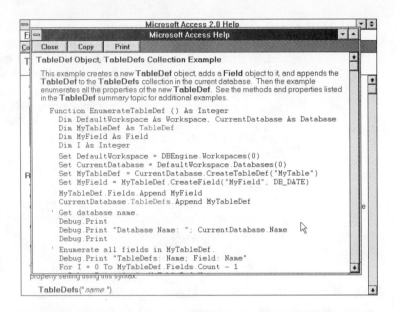

FIGURE 12-1 Sample Access Basic code provided through Access' help

How can I slow down my Function procedure so I can find errors?

You can execute a Function or Sub procedure one line at a time. To do this, add breakpoints to your procedure. *Breakpoints* tell Access to stop executing the macro just before their line of code. After Access stops executing the code, you can choose to execute the lines one at a time. To place a breakpoint on a line of your code:

1. Move to a line in the procedure such as the first Dim statement.

2. Click the Breakpoint toolbar button, shown here. You can choose Toggle Breakpoint from the Run menu or press F9 instead.

3. Open the Immediate Window by clicking the Immediate Window toolbar button, shown here, or by choosing Immediate Window from the View menu.

Step Into

Step Over

4. Type **?** *FunctionName***()** and press ENTER. For a Sub procedure, don't enter the parentheses. The Step Into and Step Over toolbar buttons, shown here, become bold.

5. Click the Step Into or Step Over button to step through the procedure. Step Into executes one line at a time. Step Over does, too, except that a call to a subroutine or function is treated as a single step.

As an example, Figure 12-2 shows the entry in the Immediate Window that runs the PCase Function procedure. Since the first statement is a breakpoint, Access performs this entire procedure one line at a time. The line of code with a border is the one Access performs when you click the Step Into button.

Tech Tip: You can have Access display the current values of your variables in the Immediate Window while debugging a Function or Sub procedure. To do this, enter **Debug.Print** followed by the name of the variable in the procedure. Then, when Access performs that line in the procedure, the value of the variable appears in the Immediate Window.

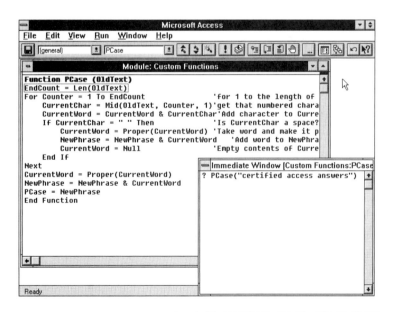

FIGURE 12-2   Showing the procedure as Access performs it one step at a time

What is the Variant data type?

The Variant data type is a special kind of data type in Access Basic. Unlike the other data types, which can only hold a certain data format, Variant variables can hold numbers, strings, dates, and nulls. Variant is the default data type in Access Basic and is useful in making your module more flexible. Its advantages are that you do not need to declare a data type and you can switch from one type to another. The disadvantage is that it uses more memory.

When do I use the Variant data type?

Use the Variant data type when you are not sure which data type you will be working with, or when you know that a variable will have more than one type of data.

What is the difference between a Sub procedure and a Function procedure?

A *Sub* procedure is a routine that carries out an operation. Unlike a Function procedure, a Sub procedure cannot return a value. *Function* procedures can return values and be used in expressions. Function procedures can be used at any other place where you would use one of Access' built-in functions. Function procedures include a statement that assigns a value to the function's name. Figure 12-3 shows both a Function procedure and a Sub procedure.

Tech Tip: The easy way to remember the difference is whether the procedure returns a value. If it does, it is a Function procedure. If it doesn't, it's a Sub procedure.

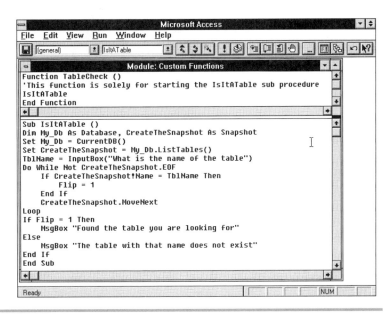

FIGURE 12-3   Module window showing a Sub procedure and a Function procedure

Where can I put functions that I have written?

You can put the functions you create and Access' built-in functions in modules in several locations in your databases. These locations include

- The ControlSource property of an unbound text box on a form or report where it provides the contents of the text box.

- An event property of a form or report. For example, assign a function as the OnClick property of a command button control to have the function perform when you click the command button.

- The Field/Expression column of the Sorting and Grouping dialog box used to sort and group data in a report.

- The Field line in a query's QBE grid where it provides the entry for that field in the query's datasheet.

- The Criteria line in a query's QBE grid where it tells Access which data to choose with the query.

- The Update To line in an update query where it supplies the new table entry made by the query.

- The Condition column of a macro where it chooses when to perform a macro action.

- The Expression argument of a SetValue macro action where it sets what the Item argument equals.

- The Function Name argument in a RunCode macro action.

- Another Function or Sub procedure.

My code is stuck in an infinite loop. How do I stop it?

Press CTRL+BREAK to stop executing a procedure.

How did Access Basic improve between Access 1.*x* and 2.0?

Access Basic in Access 2.0 has several enhancements. These enhancements include the following:

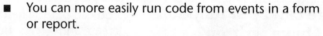

- You can more easily run code from events in a form or report.

- Forms and reports can store the procedures in a module that is part of the form or report.

- You can set the properties of an open form or report without switching to Design view first.

- Access Basic 2.0 has Data Access objects to include groups of objects in the database.

- Access Basic procedures can manipulate OLE objects in other applications.

- Access Basic has more methods and built-in functions to make the tasks that you wanted to do in Access Basic 1.*x* easier to do.

Tech Tip: When you convert a database, Access makes some of the changes for you. You may also see warnings about an invalid argument.

Table 12-1 shows several Access 1.*x* statements, functions, methods, and properties that you should replace with the Access 2.0 equivalents to make your procedures work better.

Why is Access ignoring my control's input mask after I added an Access Basic function to assign a value to the control?

If you use Access Basic or a macro to assign a value to a control or field that has an input mask, Access ignores the input mask. Therefore, include the effect of the input mask in the Access Basic code or macro.

Access 1.*x* Feature	Improved Access 2.0 Feature
BeginTrans statement	BeginTrans method of the Workspace object
CommitTrans statement	CommitTrans method of the Workspace object
Rollback statement	Rollback method of the Workspace object
CreateDynaset	OpenRecordset method of the Database object
CreateSnapshot	OpenRecordset method of the Database object
OpenTable	OpenRecordset method of the Database object
CurrentDB() function	Databases(0) element of the Databases collection of the Workspace object
DeleteQueryDef method	Delete method of the QueryDefs collection
ExecuteSQL method	Execute method of the Database object
Fields property of the Index object	Fields collection of the Index object
ListFields method	Fields collection of the object
ListIndexes method	Indexes collection of the TableDef object or the Recordset of type Table object
ListParameters method	Parameters collection of the QueryDef object
ListTables method	TableDefs or QueryDefs collection of the Database object
OpenDatabase function	OpenDatabase method of the Workspace object
Dynaset form property	RecordsetClone property of a form

TABLE 12-1   Access 1.*x* features to replace with better Access 2.0 features

What is a Recordset?

Recordsets represent data from a base table or the result of a query. Access has three types of Recordsets: tables, dynasets, and snapshots.

Can you view two procedures at once?

Yes. Choose Split <u>W</u>indow from the <u>V</u>iew menu. Access divides the Module window in half. At this point, both halves of the window show the same procedure. You can switch either half to show another procedure. You can drag the split bar that divides the two halves up or down to change how much of the window each part uses. Figure 12-3 shows a Module window split between two procedures.

Tech Tip: The split bar appears at the top of the Module window when it isn't split. Dragging this split bar down is another way to split a window.

I have a line of code that is very long. Can I continue it on the next line?

No. There is no continuation character in Access Basic.

What is an event procedure?

An event procedure is a Sub procedure associated with a particular event property on a form or report. When the particular event occurs, Access calls the event procedure. All the event procedures for a form or report are saved with the form or report. Access assigns event procedures specific names describing the control and the event to which the procedure is assigned. For example, the event procedure in Figure 12-4 is the procedure run when you click the control named Button0.

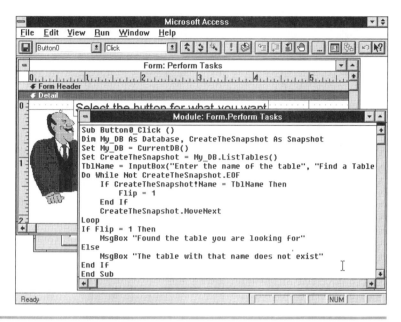

FIGURE 12-4 Event procedure assigned to an event on a form

What is the difference between the Or and Xor operators?

The difference between these two operators is that *Or* is inclusive, while *Xor* is exclusive.

For example, suppose you are comparing A and B. Since *Xor* is exclusive, **A Xor B** is true only if A meets the criteria and B does not, or B meets the criteria and A does not. *Xor* is true only when just one of the two comparisons is true.

On the other hand, **A Or B** is true if A meets the criteria whether or not B does. *Or* is true when either one or both of the comparisons are true.

How can I set the RecordSource property of a form at runtime?

Use the Me property to specify the current table or query for the RecordSource property. An example is

```
Me.RecordSource="New Record Source"
```

New Record Source represents the table or query that the form or report opened with this setting will use.

Can I delete a table in a Function procedure?

Access 2.0 has a Delete method that deletes records, fields, indexes, or tables. When you delete the TableDef collection that represents a table, the table definition and the data in that table are deleted. The following Access Basic code deletes a table named Table1.

For example:

```
Dim MyTable As TableDef, MyDatabase As Database
Set MyDatabase = DBEngine(0)(0)
Set MyTable = MyDatabase.TableDefs("Table1")
MyDatabase.TableDefs.Delete MyTable.Name
```

In these Access Basic statements, the MyTable variable contains a table definition, and the MyDatabase variable contains the database object. The Set MyDatabase statement assigns the current database to the MyDatabase variable. The Set MyTable statement assigns the Table1 table to the MyTable variable. The final statement performs the Delete method on the table definitions that are part of the database represented by the MyDatabase variable. It deletes Table1, which contains the results of MyTable.Name.

I printed a Word 6.0 document by using the DDE example from page 146 of the *Introduction to Programming* book that came with Access 1.1. I just converted to Access 2.0 and this code gives me errors. What happened?

In Access 2.0, you can now use OLE automation to access and manipulate another application's objects outside that application.

This means that Access Basic can more easily run another application. The code can be much shorter and simpler. This code performs the same function with a linked OLE object as your old code:

```
Dim WordObj As Object
Set WordObj = CreateObject("Word.Basic")
WordObj.FileOpen "C:\WINWORD\OLE1.DOC"
WordObj.FilePrint
WordObj.FileClose (1)
```

This code opens the document in Word, prints the document, and closes the application. You can replace the "C:\WINWORD\OLE1.DOC" with the name of the Word file. You can also use a variable name to set the filename when executing the code. The document appears in a separate Word window rather than as part of the Access window, thereby allowing you to edit the document in Word.

Tech Tip: You may also be able to get the results you want with the SendObject and OutputTo actions. These actions take Access data and send it to Excel and Word for Windows.

How do I replace Forms! [*Form Name*] in my code with the contents of a variable?

You can replace Forms![*Form Name*] in your code with a variable name. The following example shows how to do this using MyVar as the name of the variable that will equal an acceptable form name.

```
Dim MyVar as String
Let MyVar = "FormName"
```

Now you can replace Forms![*Form Name*] with Forms(MyVar).

Why doesn't my Database window show the TableDef object in the list of tables?

Access does not automatically refresh the Database window when you create TableDef objects. To see the newly created TableDef object in the Database window, choose another list of objects, such as queries, and then switch back to the list of tables. The Database window then refreshes its list and the TableDef object appears.

When I reference the index on the primary key of my table, I get the error message "*index name* isn't an index in this table." How do I reference this index?

The reason for the error is that the index for the primary key uses the name PrimaryKey rather than using the name of the field on which it is based. When you refer to the primary key index of a table, use the following syntax:

```
TBL.Index = "PrimaryKey"
```

How do I display a global variable from a module on a form?

First, you need a procedure that returns the value of the global variable, similar to this one:

```
Function ReturnMyGlobal() as Integer
ReturnMyGlobal = Global1
Function Sub
```

This example assumes that the global variable you want returned has the name Global1 and it is an integer. Next, you need to put a reference to this procedure on the form. You can do this by entering = **ReturnMyGlobal( )** for the ControlSource property of an unbound text box. If the global variable is not an integer, as the preceding example assumes, replace Integer in the Function statement with the appropriate data type.

Can an Access Basic procedure create a form or report?

Yes. The way to create a form or report by using Access Basic is to use the CreateForm or CreateReport function. These functions create a form or report that is empty except for what the template places on the design document. The syntax for these functions is

```
CreateForm(database, formtemplate)
CreateReport(database, reporttemplate)
```

Database is the name identifying the database that contains the template. *Formtemplate* or *reporttemplate* is the name of the form or report template to use. Note that if you omit *database*, Access uses the current database. If the form or report template is invalid or missing, Access Basic uses the form or report template specified in the Options dialog box. Once the procedure creates the form or report, other Access Basic statements can add controls and make property changes.

What code do I add to a form to change the RecordSource property while the form is still open?

You can add this line to your program:

```
Me.RecordSource = Table name, query name or SQL statement
```

You can also do this in a macro by adding the SetValue action. For the Item argument, enter Forms![*Form Name*].RecordSource. For the Expression argument, enter the table name, query name, or SQL statement.

How do I reset all of my global variables at once?

The most direct approach to this problem is to create a function like this one:

```
Sub ResetMyGlobals()
Global1 = 0
Global2 = 0
...
End Sub
```

Now you only need to call the function to reset your global variables.

Why can't I use DoCmd in Access Basic to delete a module?

You can't use DoCmd DeleteObject "Module", "*Module Name*" to delete a module. If you try, you get the message "Illegal function call" or "Duplicate Definition." Instead, you have to use a macro to delete the module.

Tech Tip: The DoCmd command can perform macro actions (except for AddMenu, MsgBox, RunApp, RunCode, SendKeys, SetValue, StopAllMacros, and StopMacro). After DoCmd, enter the macro action followed by the macro's arguments using commas to separate the arguments.

Can Access Basic add a user and set the user's permissions?

Yes, you can add users and set permissions with Access Basic. In Access Basic, use the CreateUser method. This method creates a User object. An example of this method is this code:

```
Dim MyWorkspace As Workspace
Dim MyUser As User
Set MyWorkspace = DBEngine.Workspaces(0)
Set MyUser = MyWorkspace.CreateUser("Faith Kleinert",
          "ALPHABET", "Safe")
```

This code defines the MyWorkspace variable as a Workspace object and MyUser as a User object. Then the first Set statement sets the MyWorkspace variable equal to the current Workspace object. The second Set statement sets the value of MyUser to the User object created with the CreateUser method. This method created a user account for Faith Kleinert. This user account has a PID (Personal Identifier) of ALPHABET and a password of Safe.

Once you create the user, you can add the user to a group. For example, the following statements add this user to the Top Level group:

```
MyWorkspace.Groups![Top Level].Users.Append MyUser
MyWorkspace.Users![Faith Kleinert].Groups.Refresh
```

How can my procedure change the application name in the Microsoft Access title bar?

You can create a function that changes the application title bar in Access, and then add this function where you want the title bar changed. To create this function, you first need to place the following code on the Declarations page of a module:

```
Declare Function FindWindow% Lib "User" (ByVal lpClassName As
    Any, ByVal lpWindowName As Any)
Declare Sub SetWindowText Lib "User" (ByVal hwind%, ByVal
    lpString$)
```

The first statement declares a reference to an external Function procedure named FindWindow% in the User dynamic link library (the USER.EXE file in your \WINDOWS\SYSTEM directory). This function has two arguments that this statement identifies as lpClassName and lpWindowName. They can be any data type. When you use the function, Access passes the two arguments as values rather than addresses. Passing arguments by addresses would let the function modify the value of the variables. Each Declare statement must be completely entered on a single line.

The second statement declares a Sub procedure named SetWindowText also in the User dynamic link library. This Sub procedure has two arguments: one is an integer and the other a string. Their data type is identified by the % and $ characters at the end of their name.

Next, in the same module, create the following function:

```
Function SetCaption (NewWindowText$)
Dim hwind%
hwind% = FindWindow%("OMAIN", 0&)
Call SetWindowText(hwind%, NewWindowText$)
End Function
```

This function accepts text supplied when you perform this Function procedure. The FindWindow% Function procedure, run from the dynamic link library, returns the value of the Access application window. The Call statement executes the SetWindowText Sub procedure by using the window number and the new text for the title bar as arguments.

Now when you want to change the text of the application title bar, use the SetCaption Function procedure you have just created. An example is typing **? SetCaption ("Gift Idea Catalog")** in the Immediate Window. You can also add **SetCaption("*Text for window title*")** as the contents of an event procedure you assign to a form or report. This makes the application title bar match the form or report name.

Miscellaneous Questions

This chapter addresses some of the miscellaneous problems you may encounter with Access that don't fit into the other chapters of this book. However, if you can't find an answer here, you can also check Access' online Help system. The following Frustration Busters box has tips for navigating Help. Once you familiarize yourself with it, Help can provide you with all sorts of useful tips, tricks, and solutions.

FRUSTRATION BUSTERS!

Access' online Help system is your first line of defense against questions or problems. You can start Help in several ways:

- Press F1 to display either the Microsoft Access Help Contents screen, or a topic about the current dialog box or error message.

- Click the Help toolbar button, and then choose a command or click an item to display a Help topic about that command or item.

- Click the Help button in a dialog box to display information about the available options.

- Right-click something and choose Help from the shortcut menu for assistance on what you are pointing to.

- Choose a command from the Help menu:

    a. *Contents* opens the Help window to the Microsoft Access Help Contents topic.

    b. *Search* opens the Help window and presents a Search dialog box to find a particular topic.

    c. *Cue Cards* opens the Microsoft Access Cue Cards that walk you through Access features using your own data.

    d. *Technical Support* provides information about what to do when you have a question that the online Help can't answer.

    e. *About Microsoft Access* provides information about Access and your system.

The Help application displays *topics,* which are windows of information about a given item or problem. You have two main ways of moving between topics in the Help application to find the one that answers your question.

- Click text that appears underlined or green, called a *hot spot,* to move to that particular topic. If a hot spot is underlined with a dotted line, selecting it displays a pop-up box with an explanation or definition instead of moving you to another topic.

■ Click the <u>S</u>earch button to open the Search dialog box and look for topics related to a specific keyword.

The Access Basic or Examples hot spots open a separate window to show sample macros or procedures. To close this window, double-click its Control-menu box. To exit the Help application itself, choose E<u>x</u>it from its <u>F</u>ile menu or double-click its Control-menu box. If you exit Access without exiting the Help application, Access closes it for you.

How can I display the toolbox in Design view when <u>T</u>oolbox is dimmed in the <u>V</u>iew menu?

This command isn't available because Access' built-in toolbars are turned off. To make the toolbox and other toolbars available again:

1. Choose <u>O</u>ptions from the <u>V</u>iew menu.

2. Choose General under <u>C</u>ategory.

3. Under <u>I</u>tems, make sure that Built-In Toolbars Available is set to Yes.

4. Select OK.

Can I hide all built-in toolbars and still use the Toolbox and Palette?

No. In Access 2.0, the Palette and Toolbox are built-in toolbars. The only way you can hide them and still have their features is

Tech Tip: The toolbar you create has the name of Custom Toolbar 1. You can rename it by choosing Tool**b**ars from the **V**iew menu, highlighting the toolbar in the Toolbars list box, and selecting Rena**m**e. Type the new name, and then select OK and Close.

to add their buttons to a custom toolbar. To create your own toolbar:

1. Choose Tool**b**ars from the **V**iew menu or right-click any toolbar.

2. Choose **C**ustomize. Access displays the dialog box shown in Figure 13-1.

3. Select a category from the **C**ategories list box that includes a button you want in your new toolbar.

4. Drag the button to an empty area of the screen. Access creates a custom toolbar containing that button.

5. Continue dragging buttons from the Buttons section in the Customize dialog box to the new toolbar.

6. When you are finished, click Close to close the dialog box and save the toolbar.

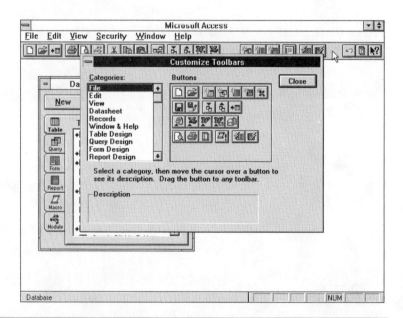

FIGURE 13-1 Customize Toolbars dialog box for changing and creating toolbars

What's an easy way to view the query that the report or form is based on?

While in the form or report's Design view, display the property sheet. If you select the RecordSource property, a Build button (a set of ellipses or three periods) appears. If you click it, the query the report or form is based on opens in Design view.

Can I use an SQL statement as the record source for a form?

Yes, a form or report can get its data from an SQL statement. The form or report includes the same records as a query designed with the same SQL statement. You can type the SQL statement in the Record Source property of a form or report. You can also click the Build button at the end of this property's field to open a Query Builder: SQL Statement window. Here you can use the QBE grid to create a query and view the results of its SQL statement. When the correct records are selected, close the window. Access places the SQL statement that represents the query into the Record Source property.

How can I speed up a report or form based on a crosstab query?

Using fixed column headings improves the performance of forms and reports based on crosstab queries. To create fixed column headings, display the property sheet for the query. In the Column Headings property, type the heading entries for the crosstab query, separated with commas. Supplying the column headings only works if the query has the same column headings every time you run the query.

Why are the form and report Wizards dimmed so I can't select one?

There are several possible reasons for this:

- The database has no tables or queries. You can't use these Wizards since you have no data that they can use.

As soon as you create a table, you can create forms and reports with the Wizards.

■ The MSACC20.INI file is missing information in its [Libraries] section. To fix this problem:

1. Open the MSACC20.INI file in a text editor.

2. Find the [Libraries] section.

3. Verify that the following entry appears:

```
[Libraries]
wzfrmrpt.mda = rw
```

■ The Wizards may not be loaded. To check this:

1. Choose Add-ins in the File menu, and then choose Add-in Manager. The Add-in Manager lists the add-ins you can load.

2. Highlight Form and Report Wizards in the Available Libraries list box and select Install.

3. Select Close to leave the Add-in Manager.

■ The Wizards may not be installed. This is often the problem if you did not install all of Access. You can install the Wizards with these steps:

1. Switch to the Program Manager and display the program group containing your Access icons.

2. Double-click the MS Access Setup icon.

Tech Tip: If you do not have a MS Access Setup icon, you can start Setup by inserting the first Access installation disk in drive A, choosing Run from the File menu, typing **A:\SETUP** in the Command Line box, and clicking OK.

3. Click Add/Remove. The Options list box displays check boxes for the different parts of the Access program.

4. Select the Wizards check box. You can also select Change Option to select which Wizards you are installing, and then select OK to return to the Maintenance Installation dialog box.

5. Click Continue.

6. When prompted, insert the requested Access Setup disks.

7. Click OK when Setup finishes installing the desired components.

 # Can I modify the form or report that the Wizards create?

Yes, you can use the Add-in Manager to change the settings for a Wizard:

1. Choose Add-ins from the File menu while in the Database window and choose Add-in Manager. The Add-in Manager dialog box lists the available Wizards.

2. Select Form and Report Wizards from the Available Libraries list box.

3. Select the Customize button. At this point, you can choose which form or report Wizard you want to modify.

4. Choose the part of the Wizard you want to change. Your choices include

   a. *Customize Form Wizard Styles*   This changes the appearance of the form styles. Each style available to a form Wizard has its own settings for how the text box and labels look.

   b. *Customize Report Wizard Styles*   This changes the appearance of the report styles. Each style available to a report Wizard has its own settings for how the text box and labels look.

   c. *Customize AutoForm*   This selects the form style and how the fields are arranged on the form created when you click the AutoForm toolbar button.

   d. *Customize AutoReport*   This selects the report style, how the fields are arranged, orientation, and line spacing on the report created when you click the AutoReport toolbar button.

   e. *Customize Mailing Label Sizes*   This adds and alters custom label sizes that supplement the ones built into Access.

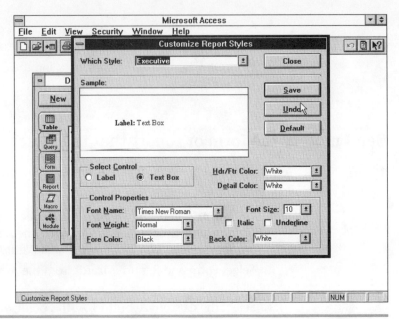

FIGURE 13-2 Dialog box to change how the reports created with a Wizard appear

5. Once you choose one of these, you can alter that Wizard. Figure 13-2 shows the dialog box you use to set the appearance of text boxes and labels of a report created with one of the report Wizards.

6. Select OK or Close to close the dialog box.

7. Select Close to close the Add-in Manager.

How do I capitalize the first letter of each word in a Text field?

You can create a Function procedure that capitalizes text. Then you can use this function as if it is one of Access' built-in functions. To create this procedure, type the following into a module:

```
Function Capitalize (Word As Variant) As String
Dim Temp As String, C As String, OldC As String, X As Integer
If IsNull(Word) Then
    Exit Function
Else
    Temp = CStr(LCase(Word))
    OldC = " "
    For X = 1 To Len(Temp)
        C = Mid(Temp, X, 1)
        If C >= "a" And C <= "z" And
        (OldC < "a" Or OldC > "z") Then
            Mid(Temp, X, 1) = UCase(C)
        End If
        OldC = C
    Next X
    Capitalize = Temp
End If
End Function
```

In the query or ControlSource property, change the field name to:

```
= Capitalize([Text Field Name])
```

For example, = Capitalize("245 cory street") returns 245 Cory Street and = Capitalize("microsoft access support") returns Microsoft Access Support.

Can I create a Function procedure that will calculate a person's age?

Yes, if you know a person's date of birth, you can create a Function procedure that will subtract the person's birthday from today's date and convert the number of days between the two dates into years. You can create this procedure by typing the following into a module:

```
Function HowOld (DOB As String) As Long
Dim Birthday As Double
Birthday = CVDate(DOB)
HowOld = Fix(DateDiff("d", Birthday, Date) / 365.25)
End Function
```

Within this procedure, DOB represents the date of birth. You can use this function just like you use Access' built-in functions. For example, a control in a form can have a ControlSource property of = HowOld([Date Of Birth]). If Date Of Birth equals 7/5/66 and today is 7/14/94, this control displays 28.

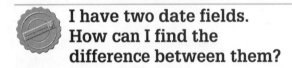 **I have two date fields. How can I find the difference between them?**

To find the difference between two dates, you simply subtract them, as in **=[First Date Field]-[Second Date Field]**. You can enter this expression as a calculated field in a query, as a calculated control in a form or report, or as a calculation in an Access Basic procedure.

This calculation returns the difference between the dates as the number of days between the two dates. You can also use functions like Month() or Year() to return the number of months or years in the difference between two dates. For example, you could enter **= Month([First Date Field]-[Second Date Field])** to determine the number of months between these two dates.

You can also use the DateDiff() function. This function returns a part of the date depending on the interval you provide for the function's first argument. Table 13-1 lists the possible interval entries. As an example of this function at work, you can enter **= DateDiff("yyyy",[First Date Field],[Second Date Field])** as the ControlSource property for an unbound control in a form or report. This control will display the difference in years between the two dates. To display a different interval, replace **"yyyy"** with another entry from Table 13-1.

Interval	Result
"yyyy"	The number of years difference between the two dates
"q"	The number of quarters difference between the two dates
"m"	The number of months difference between the two dates
"y"	The number of days difference between the two dates
"d"	The number of days difference between the two dates
"w"	The number of weekdays difference between the two dates
"ww"	The number of weeks difference between the two dates
"h"	The number of hours difference between the two times
"n"	The number of minutes difference between the two times
"s"	The number of seconds difference between the two times

TABLE 13-1   Possible intervals for the DateDIff function

Can I find the size of a text file in bytes?

You can create a procedure that opens the text file in Access Basic and then uses the LOF function to return the file's size in bytes. A procedure that performs this on a text file named CONSTANT.TXT might look like:

```
Function Size_Of_File ()
Dim Filesize As Integer
Open "CONSTANT.TXT" For Input As #1
Filesize = LOF(1)
Close #1
Size_Of_File = Filesize
End Function
```

How can I get to my library databases so I can debug them?

Library databases are usually databases of Access procedures that you want available in other databases. Libraries act behind the scenes to provide features that appear to be part of Access. You usually don't see these databases. However, if you create your own, you may need to view and edit them.

In Access 1.*x*, you had to take a library out of MSACCESS.INI to fix it. It's much easier to get to these libraries in Access 2.0. Now just add the following entry to your MSACC20.INI file in the [OPTIONS] section:

```
[OPTIONS]
DebugLibraries=True
```

This line lets you get to your library procedures. To display one of the procedures from a library procedure so you can edit them and test how they work:

1. Open a Module window for one of your databases.
2. Choose Procedures from the View menu.
3. Select a library database from the Databases drop-down list box.
4. Choose the module and procedure to modify from the Modules and the Procedures list boxes.
5. Select OK. The open Module window shows the module from the selected library.

How do I round my numbers to a specific number of decimal places?

You can create a Round function that rounds a number to a set number of decimal places. If you have used rounding functions in spreadsheet applications, you are already familiar with how to use this one. To create this function, type the following into a module:

```
Function Round (Value As Variant, Decimals As Integer)
If Decimals >= 0 Then
    Round = Int(Value * 10 ^ Decimals + .5) / 10 ^ Decimals
Else
    MsgBox "Invalid amount of decimal places for this
function.", 48, "Round UDF"
    Round = Value
End If
End Function
```

You can use this procedure just like Access' built-in functions. In the query or control source where you would usually refer to just the field, enter the following:

```
= Round([Number Field Name], x)
```

X represents the number of decimal places to use for rounding. For example, Round(123.45678, 2) will return 123.46 and Round(87.654321, 3) will return 87.654.

How can I convert a number to its cardinal equivalent?

You can create a Function procedure that takes a number and converts it to a string with text like "st" or "th" after it. To create this function, type the following into a module:

```
Function Cardinal (Num As Double)
Dim NumPart As String   ' NumPart to contain the number's suffix
Cardinal = Num   ' Assign the value of Num to Cardinal
If Num > 0 Then   ' Add a cardinal suffix when Num > 0
    NumPart = Right(Num, 1)   ' Get the last digit from Num
    Select Case Val(NumPart)
' Choose which suffix based on the last digit
        Case 1
            Cardinal = Num & "st"
' When Num = 1 Cardinal equals Num and "st"
        Case 2
            Cardinal = Num & "nd"
' When Num = 2 Cardinal equals Num and "nd"
        Case 3
            Cardinal = Num & "rd"
' When Num = 3 Cardinal equals Num and "rd"
        Case Else
            Cardinal = Num & "th"
' When Num = 4 Cardinal equals Num and "th"
    End Select
End If
If Val(Right(Num, 2)) > 10 And Val(Right(Num, 2)) < 14 Then
    Cardinal = Num & "th"
' Replace 11st, 12nd, and 13rd with 11th, 12th & 13th
End If
End Function
```

In the query or ControlSource property where you would usually refer to just the field, enter the following:

```
= Cardinal([Field Name])
```

This only works for numbers greater than zero. Any number less than zero entered into the function is returned without modification. As examples of this procedure's output,

= Cardinal(1) returns 1st, = Cardinal(14) returns 14th, and
= Cardinal(-23) returns -23.

How can I transfer data from a form to an Excel spreadsheet and get the name for the workbook from the form?

The form has a macro that handles exporting the data in the form to an Excel workbook. This macro has the TransferSpreadsheet action. However, instead of a workbook name for the File Name argument, enter **=Forms![*Form Name*]![*Control Name*]** where the *Control Name* is the name of the form's control that contains the name for the workbook file.

I am only seeing every other bar label in my form or report's graph. How do I move the ticks apart so that I can see all of my labels?

Microsoft Graph 5.0 does not have an option to increase the space between ticks. To see all of your labels, click on the Category (X) axis, choose Alignment, and choose an alignment option that shows the labels on their sides. This alignment gives the graph more room along the axis, so you can see all of your labels on the graph. Figure 13-3 shows a graph where the labels are rotated. If you do this and still can't see all the labels, you must lengthen the graph.

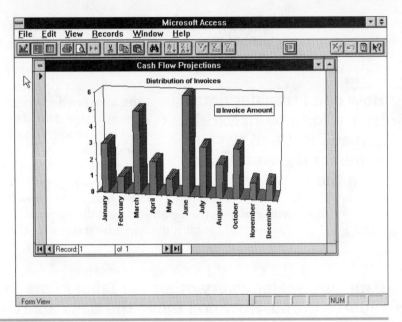

FIGURE 13-3 Graph using a different alignment for labels so you can see all of them

How do I know when to use the exclamation point or the period in an expression?

You use the exclamation point before anything you can name yourself and a period before anything that Microsoft Access names. For example, form names and control names have an exclamation point before them. Properties have a period.

Tech Tip: Let the Expression Builder answer this question for you. When you select a control or property here, the Expression Builder adds all of the punctuation for you as well as names of objects and controls.

Index

Numbers and Symbols

&, 168, 225, 228-229
* alignment character, 52
* wildcard characters
  in the Field row of the QBE
    grid, 88
  in IIf function, 96
  in parameter queries, 99,
    100, 101
<=> button, 107
<, for entering uppercase
  letters, 180
  in validation rules, 171
< Format property, for forcing
  lowercase display, 45
>, for entering lowercase
  letters, 180
> Format property, for forcing
  uppercase display, 45
! alignment character, 53
' (apostrophe), starting Access
  Basic commands, 232
! (exclamation point), in
  expressions, 264
. (period), in expressions, 264

- (hyphen), for creating lines in
  custom menus, 229
\ (backslash) operator, for
  integer division, 87
∞ (infinity sysmbol), in the
  Relationships window, 68
| (pipe or vertical bar), as the
  default value for a field, 52

A

Access
  backing up, 22
  importing Lotus Notes files
    into, 204
  installing, 15-17
  installing on compressed
    drives, 13
  installing on a network, 18
  installing on a Novell
    network, 35
  networks supported by, 14
  and OLE, 204
  online help in, 233-234
  reinstalling, 14
Access Basic, 231
  and code continuation, 240

If you would like to **speak to the experts** who wrote this book, **call**

Corporate Software's

Microsoft Access®

answer line!

Have we answered all your questions?

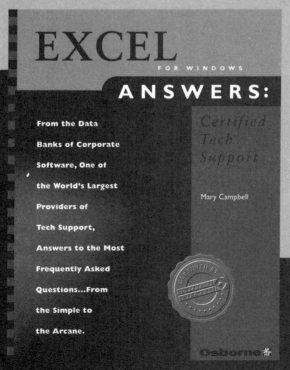

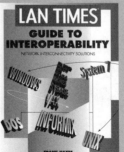

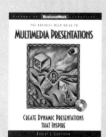

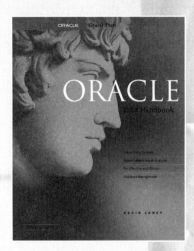

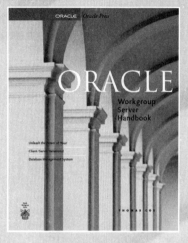

Think Fast
PASSING LANE AHEAD

Lotus Notes Answers: Certified Tech Support
by Polly Russell Kornblith
$16.95 U.S.A.
ISBN: 0-07-882055-3

What's the quickest route to tech support? Osborne's new Certified Tech Support series. Developed in conjunction with Corporate Software Inc., one of the largest providers of tech support fielding more than 200,000 calls a month, Osborne delivers the most authoritative question and answer books available anywhere. Speed up your computing and stay in the lead with answers to the most frequently asked end-user questions—from the simple to the arcane. And watch for more books in the series.

BC640SL

ORDER BOOKS DIRECTLY FROM OSBORNE/McGRAW-HILL

For a complete catalog of Osborne's books, call 510-549-6600 or write to us at 2600 Tenth Street, Berkeley, CA 94710

☎ **Call Toll-Free: 1-800-822-8158**
24 hours a day, 7 days a week in U.S. and Canada

✉ **Mail this order form to:**
McGraw-Hill, Inc.
Customer Service Dept.
P.O. Box 547
Blacklick, OH 43004

📠 **Fax this order form to:**
1-614-759-3644

💻 **EMAIL**
7007.1531@COMPUSERVE.COM
COMPUSERVE GO MH

Ship to:

Name _____

Company _____

Address _____

City / State / Zip _____

Daytime Telephone: _____
(We'll contact you if there's a question about your order.)

ISBN #	BOOK TITLE	Quantity	Price	Total
0-07-88				
0-07-88				
0-07-88				
0-07-88				
0-07-88				
0-07088				
0-07-88				
0-07-88				
0-07-88				
0-07-88				
0-07-88				
0-07-88				
0-07-88				
0-07-88				

	Shipping & Handling Charge from Chart Below	
	Subtotal	
	Please Add Applicable State & Local Sales Tax	
	TOTAL	

Shipping & Handling Charges

Order Amount	U.S.	Outside U.S.
Less than $15	$3.50	$5.50
$15.00 - $24.99	$4.00	$6.00
$25.00 - $49.99	$5.00	$7.00
$50.00 - $74.99	$6.00	$8.00
$75.00 - and up	$7.00	$9.00

Occasionally we allow other selected companies to use our mailing list. If you would prefer that we not include you in these extra mailings, please check here: ☐

METHOD OF PAYMENT

☐ Check or money order enclosed (payable to Osborne/McGraw-Hill)

☐ AMERICAN EXPRESS   ☐ DISCOVER   ☐ MasterCard   ☐ VISA

Account No. [ ][ ][ ][ ][ ][ ][ ][ ][ ][ ][ ][ ][ ][ ][ ]

Expiration Date _____

Signature _____

In a hurry? Call 1-800-822-8158 anytime, day or night, or visit your local bookstore.

Thank you for your order   Code BC640SL